Sunset Home Remodeling Guide to
Paneling, Painting & Wallpapering

*By the Editors of Sunset Books
and Sunset Magazine*

Cedar paneling
*Handsomely paneled wall is
striking accent in room where
other walls are painted. These
3½-inch-wide cedar board strips
can form any of several patterns;
installation is with paneling
adhesive.*

Lane Publishing Co. • Menlo Park, California

They joined the team . . .

Collecting the key elements of paneling, painting, and wallpapering between the covers of a single book calls for teamwork. We are grateful to the following people for their time, effort, and care in helping to gather factual information and organize it into its final form: Sherry Gellner, Lee Carrau, Donald W. Vandervort, John Gillespie, Roger Flanagan, and Joe Seals.

A special thanks to the following for their generosity in sharing their experience and knowledge with us: Robert Cheney (Wallpapers to Go), Len Craig (Craig's Morwear Paint Distributors, Inc.), Don Douglas (Albert Van Luit & Co.), Rodney Jones (Ameritone Paint Corporation), Lee Ludke (Ludke's Menlo Paints), Helen C. Mills (Wallpapers Inc.), Gift Morton (Hubbard & Johnson Lumber Co.), and Ron Saturno (Designers Workshop).

Edited by Robert G. Bander

Special Consultant: Ray Loughlin
Design and Illustrations: Joe Seney
Cover: Photographed by Darrow M. Watt

Editor, Sunset Books: David E. Clark

Third Printing June 1977

Prepare, then pain
Painting windows becomes simple
if you first place masking tap
around pane edges

A scrubbable wallpaper
Durable vinyl wallpaper in vivid
hexagonal pattern cleans easily,
resists bathroom moisture.

CONTENTS

PANELING, PAINTING, AND WALLPAPERING: A Color Array

The following color pages show handsome wall treatments that have sprung from creative approaches to paneling, painting, and wallpapering.

If you've decided that your walls are crying out for new life but you need some inspiration to get going, these photographs may point you in the right direction. Whether your taste is traditional or touched with a fondness for the future, you'll find here fresh ideas that you can adapt to your own home.

Let color work to unify an area
Coordinating the colors of wall paint and carpeting unifies a bath-dressing room area. Interior design: Stewart Morton.

Star attraction
Brightened with orange and yellow paint, this architect-designed children's playroom is a center for activity. Chalkboard offers surface for creative fun. Interior design: Don Merkt.

How to expand walls with paint
Painted horizontal bands of varying widths help to optically widen this small bathroom. Darker color band at bottom of walls de-emphasizes unsightly basin pipes. Interior design: Orlando Diaz.

Supergraphic drama

Boldly painted supergraphic makes this fireplace wall a compelling living room focal point. Supergraphics are useful in disguising protrusions and in giving a room more apparent width or height. Interior design: MLTW/Moore, Turnbull.

Signs point the way —you can't get lost

Oversized labels painted on doors guarantee you'll exit to the outside area of your choice. Interior design: J. Paul Howe.

Painting changes mood of paneled room

Paneled living-bedroom area (right) was painted (above) to eliminate the cluttered look the room formerly had because too many
different building materials had been used in a relatively
small area. Painting also covers the uneven color of wood
paneling that did not match from piece to piece. An important
side benefit of redecorating is the brightening and visual
enlargement of the room. Interior design: Patrick Windle.

Bright colors ''push out,''
''pull in'' walls, ceiling

Bright colors applied in various
combinations can appear to
change the shape of a room. Colors
can seemingly move walls and ceilings
in and out, up and down.
Interior design: Edgar Dethlefson.

Wallpaper unifies sections

Multicolored vinyl wallpaper covers
ceiling and walls of compartmented
bathroom, visually connecting sections.
Interior design: Livingston-Thayer.

A striped wall adds interest

Color-keyed to the paneled ceiling, these
vertical stripes show that papering
a single wall can be highly decorative.
Interior design: Edgar Dethlefson.

Cloth stapled above wainscoting

Cross-striped cloth was stapled to wall at ceiling
and at wainscoting. Green grosgrain ribbon covers
staples; small tacks hold cloth to wall at seams.

Mountain scene in glazed chintz

Stylized mountain design on fabric-covered wall
lends tranquil air to bedroom. Fabric design: Jack
Lenor Larsen. Interior design: Phoebe Common.

Scenic mural wallpaper resembles fine fabric

Delicately conceived in an oriental motif, this striking wallpaper has the look of richly textured fabric. Interior design: Albert Van Luit & Co.

Wallpaper coordinates with furnishings

Many wallpapers designed for children's rooms have companion fabrics that can be used for covering mattresses, making bedspreads, upholstering furniture, or hanging as curtains.

Matching cloth for den's wall, curtain, couch

Plaid seersucker has three uses here: wall covering, curtain, and couch cover. The 45-inch-wide fabric was stapled onto the wall; wood molding at ceiling holds top edge.
Interior design: Jo Ann George.

Ceilings can be decorative

Here the ceiling has been treated as a decorative surface, papered with foil wallpaper to add novelty and top-of-the-room appeal.

Bold straw and yarn weave

Bathroom wall (left) covered in paper-backed straw and yarn weave (see detail above) exudes elegance. Paper backing shows through weave. The alternating dark and light vertical stripes on bathroom wall create a two-dimensional effect. Interior design: Churchill-Zlatunich Assoc., A.I.A.

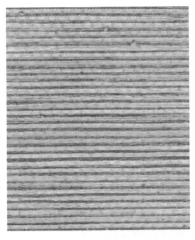

Philippine product with a subtle look: abaca

The walls of this business office (below) are covered with abaca (see detail at right). The subtly rich tones of this 30-inch-wide handwoven material enhance homes as well as professional settings. Interior design: Winfield Design.

Mylar wallpaper gives a diffused reflection

Dining room wall papered in foil reflects light and objects in a diffused manner, expands room's depth.

Blueprints come in handy

A home's blueprints offer a personal wall statement that can be decorative as well as a source of ready reference.

A color carnival of French posters

Wallpapers are manufactured that reproduce collections, such as this one containing a potpourri of French posters.

Wallpapering the door

Instead of being painted, this door is wallpapered to match the walls. Doing this can make a small room seem larger. Interior design: Carol Gordon.

Favorite prints displayed

Prints that recall a European grand tour are mounted on bathroom wall. Wood strips are used as divider frames. Interior design: Henry Hill.

Paneling with rough-textured wood creates impressive wall

Board on board vertical paneling of rough-textured wood gives this room an unmistakably rustic look. Alternately recessed boards provide eye appeal because of their light and shadow pattern. Interior design: Greg Dean, Apple Designers.

These two wall treatments harmonize

Placing wallpaper and paneling close together can create an attractive area if patterns are not too busy. Oak floor planking covers both wall and door.

Paneling brightened by light stain

Though wood paneling can sometimes darken a room, a bright, airy quality has been maintained here by the generous use of glass and by the light stain applied to the paneling.

Leather squares

The decorative touch gained by gluing leather squares to this door could also be achieved with squares of wood or some other material. Interior design: Henry Hill.

Plywood comes with saw-cut grooves

Exterior plywood siding comes in many patterns; this one has closely spaced grooves.

Herringbone pattern of wood and mirror strips

Spectacular wall treatment in living-dining area comes from herringbone design of alternating 1 by 6-inch rough-sawn cedar painted white and lapped over ¼ by 4-inch mirror strips. Interior design: J. Paul Howe

Rustic herringbone paneling

An increasingly popular pattern for solid board paneling is herringbone. These pecky cedar boards, used as fence boards in some areas, are suitable for paneling interiors.

Why not shingle interiors?

You can add considerable interest to a room by installing shingles on one or more interior walls. Family rooms, playrooms, halls are often good candidates for shingling.

Redwood panels supply warmth and texture

Changing the character of a previously painted wall, vertical grain redwood panels— their resawn side exposed—have been installed in a herringbone pattern. Panels were attached to the wall with contact cement. Both pieces of each herringbone were cut from one length of lumber. Interior design: Churchill-Zlatunich Assoc., A.I.A.

Paneling, painted supergraphic combined

Stylish entry hall gains its dramatic flair from a combined use of wood paneling and an expansive supergraphic. The rough-sawn cedar installed on the ceiling, wall, and front door echo the strong lines of the painted supergraphic. Interior design: J. Paul Howe.

PANELING

When it's time to settle on the style your new room's walls will have—or when you feel that the look of your old walls has outlived its appeal—then your mind will range across several wall covering possibilities.

Shall I paint? It's quick. Shall I wallpaper? It's attractive but more complicated. Or shall I cover the wall with some kind of paneling? It's elegant, but it sounds expensive.

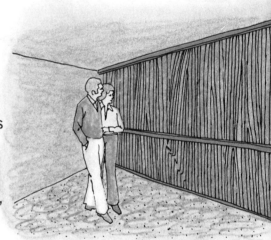

This book collects the "hows" and "wherefores" of all three wall finishing alternatives. And this first chapter focuses on paneling—telling you what it is, what it can do for you, and what steps are necessary to install it.

Let's take the mystery out of paneling. It can be elegant—or folksy. It can be expensive—or thrifty. It can be a dramatic, nonmessy, and relatively "instant" way to finish a wall.

Even if you've never paneled before, you'll find it's easy to achieve professional-looking results. Probably the only carpenter's skills you'll need are the ability to measure a room accurately and a certain talent in handling a hammer and saw.

Before you're halfway through, you may be pleasantly surprised at how simple paneling really is and how quickly the work is progressing. When you've finished, this message may come through loud and clear: paneled walls can give your room a rich new dimension.

PANELING—HANDSOME & PRACTICAL

Paneling a room, or just a wall, is a dramatic way to improve the appearance and feel of a room—and doing it need not totally absorb your cash flow. A case in point: you can panel a 12-foot wall for as little as $12.

And paneling a wall can be easy. Some wall panelings, particularly those that come in 4 by 8-foot sheets, are easier to install than some wallpapers.

This book divides paneling into two main categories: board paneling and sheet paneling. Within the sheet paneling group are hardboard, plywood, and a few other less frequently used materials. The board paneling category encompasses the various species and millings of solid wood lumber panelings.

Sheet paneling—quick and mostly inexpensive

"Sheet paneling" is a catch-all term for wall panelings that come in large panels—most commonly 4 by 8 feet. Because of its large dimensions, sheet paneling is easy to apply over large, unbroken surfaces. On the other hand, solid board paneling is easier to use where extensive handling,

maneuvering, and cutting are needed, such as around doors and windows. (Detailed instructions for installing sheet paneling begin on page 26.)

All sheet paneling products are machine made. The two main types are created either from thin layers ("veneers") of wood that are sandwiched and glued together or from compressed wood fibers and other recycled wood particles. The sandwiched type is "plywood"; the compressed panels are "hardboard."

But when you look at a wall panel, you don't *see* plywood or hardboard. What you see is the panel's surface veneer, which is treated by the manufacturer in any of a multitude of ways. Some are meant to be painted, some resemble real wood, and others are veneered with real wood that is either prefinished or meant to be finished by the buyer.

Hardboard . . . it's durable

Hardboard is tough, pliable, and water-resistant. It is sold in 4 by 8-foot sheets that range in thickness from $3/16$ inch to $3/8$ inch; $1/4$ inch is the standard.

The most common surface finishes are imitation wood; generally, these are grooved to

look like board paneling. Available are imitations of many species in highly polished, rough-sawn, and hand-hewn textures.

In addition to the wood finishes, you can find panels embossed with patterns—basketweave, wicker, and louvered, to name a few.

Generally, the more expensive panels look convincingly like the materials they are designed to imitate. The cheaper kinds have less convincing enameled finishes or thin outer surfaces of photo-printed vinyl.

For installation around tubs and showers, you can also buy hardboard with a vinyl or plastic-laminated finish that sheds water. The plastic-laminated type is the most durable. Tub and shower enclosures also come in kit form, packaged with the necessary hardware and instructions.

One familiar type of hardboard—"pegboard"—has a regular pattern of holes drilled in it for use with companion hardware hangers. This can be used effectively as a storage wall for hanging up all kinds of items.

Plywood—a grand variety of wood sheets

Plywood panels are available in many of the same simulated finishes as hardboard, but those are not where plywood shines. The better plywood panels have surface veneers of real wood—in an astounding variety. You can buy just about any species of hardwood and most of the major softwoods laminated onto the surfaces of plywood panels. In addition, plywood comes in textures ranging from highly polished to roughly textured. The wood veneers are real to the touch, and many have the warm fragrance of wood.

Standard sizes are 4 by 8 feet, but you can get some types in 4 by 9 and 4 by 10. The standard thickness of interior paneling is $1/4$ inch; because they are difficult to work with and not very durable, avoid using thinner panels. Exterior plywood sidings—ideal choices where you want rustic, rough-sawn textures—come most

Hardboard paneling *comes in many styles. The four types shown here are, from left to right, imitation wood, plastic-laminated, pegboard, and imitation brick. (Also commercially available are flat, tilelike bricks that are individually installed on a mortared surface.)*

Paneling Terms You Should Know

Backing board. Material, often gypsum wallboard, fastened to wall studs before paneling; gives paneling rigidity, offers sound insulation, and provides fire resistance.

Batten. Small-dimensioned board (often 1 by 2) frequently used to cover seams of wide boards.

Blocking. Short lengths of 2 by 4 installed horizontally between studs to provide a nailing base for paneling.

Butt seam. The joining of one panel to another without interlocking.

Chalk line. A tool used for marking a straight line across a distance (see page 66). Inexpensive chalk line strings, wound on a reel inside a container filled with chalk, are available at most hardware stores.

Combination square. A carpenter's square that includes a 45° angle and a 90° angle.

Countersinking. Using a nailset to drive nails so that their heads are slightly below the surface.

Furring. Strips of wood evenly spaced and nailed to a wall to provide a flat and plumb surface on which to install paneling.

Miter box. A tool used for guiding a saw to cut angles accurately.

Mitering. Cutting wood (usually molding) at an angle so the corner pieces fit together without showing end grain.

Molding. Plain or ornate strips of wood in many sizes and shapes used for finishing and decorating. In paneling, its practical purpose is to cover gaps where paneling meets ceiling, floor or windows, doors, and other openings.

Nominal lumber dimensions. These are the sizes you ask for when buying lumber. But the actual sizes you get—following surfacing and shrinkage—are smaller. For example, a nominal 2 by 4 is actually 1½ by 3½.

Plates, top and bottom. Horizontal 2 by 4s to which studs are attached, framing the walls in a house.

Plumb. The state of being precisely vertical (see page 23).

Scoring. Marking with a sharp tool.

Scribing. Duplicating a wall's uneven contour on the surface of a panel, using an inexpensive "scribe" or a drawing compass (see page 27).

Shimming. Placing pieces of tapered wood to fill out uneven space under furring. Shingles are often used for shimming (see page 24).

Template. Paper or thin cardboard sheet used as a pattern when marking the back of a panel for electrical outlets and other openings.

---

commonly in two thicknesses: ⅜ inch and ⅝ inch. The ⅜-inch thickness is ample for paneling.

Typical plywood panels are, from left to right, rough-sawn, imitation rough boards, hardwood-faced, prefinished "fake" wood.

Other sheet paneling materials

Following are several unusual and somewhat specialized paneling materials. Each fills a specific need; each has some advantages and some disadvantages. Though not designed as wall paneling, these materials can be used for that purpose under the right circumstances. Some of those conditions are discussed below; for installation techniques, consult your dealer.

Particleboard, chipboard, or composition panels. These names all refer to the same manufactured product: wood particles and chips compressed into a 4 by 8-foot panel. Quite heavy, it is the least expensive sheet material sold.

Unfinished panels come in thicknesses of ½, ⅝, ¾, and 1 inch. Until recently, particleboard was seldom used as paneling. But its recent use in finished furniture

has stimulated experimentation. In some areas, prefinished particleboard covered with simulated wood finishes is available, but you may have to search around to find a dealer who stocks it.

Fiberboard. With very little effort, you can poke a hole in fiberboard; it's not known for its durability and ruggedness. Though it is an unlikely candidate for such heavy action areas as family rooms, children's rooms, or hallways, fiberboard can be an inexpensive, sound-absorbing choice above wainscoting and in dens, libraries, or other areas of restrained activity.

Acoustical board. Like fiberboard, acoustical board has a limited use because of its nondurable makeup. But it reduces even more sound reverberation than fiberboard.

Panels are 1 inch thick, 2 to 4 feet wide, and available in lengths from 6 through 12 feet.

(Continued on next page)

Special-purpose paneling *materials include, from left to right, various patterns of acoustical tiles, fiberboard, a decorative chipboard, and standard particleboard.*

. . . Continued from page 19

Acoustical material also comes in "tiles" of various sizes, lock-jointed for easy installation. Typically, a tile has small holes in regular or decorative patterns on the surface. It comes with a flange for stapling to furring or with a beveled edge for application with adhesive.

Solid board paneling— a warm and real luxury

Because of texture, subtle variations in color and grain, imperfections, and natural fragrance, the friendly warmth of solid board paneling is unmatched.

TIP FROM THE PROS

When buying boards for paneling, remember that the actual size differs from the nominal size. The chart below shows standard dimensions of finished lumber.

SIZE TO ORDER	SURFACED (Actual Size)
1 x 2	¾" x 1½"
1 x 3	¾" x 2½"
1 x 4	¾" x 3½"
1 x 6	¾" x 5½"
1 x 8	¾" x 7¼"
1 x 10	¾" x 9¼"
1 x 12	¾" x 11¼"

What is solid board paneling? Just what its name implies— paneling in the form of solid boards. In some cases it is regular lumber—1 by 4s, 1 by 8s, and so forth—but most solid panelings are boards whose edges have been specially milled to overlap or fit tongue-and-groove style. The three primary millings—square edge, tongue-and-groove, and shiplap—are shown below.

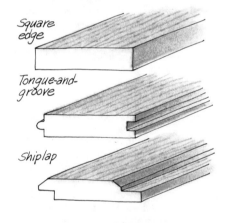

Square edge

Tongue-and-groove

Shiplap

Thickness of paneling boards ranges from a thin ⅜ inch to a more-than-adequate ⅞ inch. The standards are ½ inch and ¾ inch.

Though board widths range from 3 to 12 inches, remember that these are nominal—not actual—sizes. A 1 by 4 is not 1 inch by 4 inches. Drying, surfacing, and milling the edges reduces the size to about ¾ inch by 3½ inches (though the width depends upon the milling).

Standard lengths are 8, 10, 12, 14, and 16 feet.

No matter what the milling, boards may be rough or smooth.

The grade of wood may be "Clear" for a smooth, formal appearance or "Knotty" for a rough, informal appearance.

Solid board species

Hardwood panels are milled from such broad-leafed, deciduous trees as birch, cherry, mahogany, maple, oak, pecan, rosewood, teak, and walnut. The softwoods come from evergreen conifers (cone bearing trees)—cedar, cypress, fir, hemlock, pine, redwood, and spruce.

Barnwood, actually redwood or cedar, is a popular choice. One type is simulated; another is actually weathered, aged boards that have been salvaged from old, unpainted barns and shacks. Few lumberyards stock authentic barnwood because it is difficult to find, somewhat fragile to handle, and not uniform in size. A few firms do specialize in collecting and selling it, though. If you locate one of these firms outside your area, be prepared for the extra expense of shipping costs.

A word about cost...

Prices vary with availability. For example, redwood paneling is considerably cheaper in some western areas than it is on the east coast. In general, solid board paneling is more expensive than sheet paneling. This is particularly true of hardwoods and defect-free ("Clear") softwoods.

Unless your budget is unlimited or you are ordering a very large quantity, it isn't a good idea to choose a species or pattern that isn't stocked locally. Extras such as transportation charges and special milling can run quite high.

Installation patterns

Solid board paneling has come a long way from the days when it was almost always installed vertically. Now, many different patterns have become popular, including horizontal, diagonal, herringbone, random width and thickness, board and batten, board on gap, board on board, and strip facing patterns (see illustrations of these patterns under the discussion of each pattern beginning on page 28).

PRELIMINARY STEPS ARE IMPORTANT

Once you've decided on the kind of paneling you want to install—and the pattern—some preliminary steps remain before you climb into your working clothes.

You'll need to measure the wall or room to be paneled, estimate the number of panels you will need, buy the paneling, gather the necessary tools and equipment, prepare the room, and air the paneling correctly before installing it.

Estimating and buying materials

If the wall being paneled is a standard 8-foot height, and if you wish to panel it with sheet paneling, figuring the necessary number of panels is easy. Just measure the width of the wall in feet and divide by four. Round fractions off to the next largest number. The answer is the number of panels you need.

Unless a very large part of the wall is windows and doors, don't bother trying to figure and deduct material for them. It is much easier during installation to cut out window and door areas from the whole sheets than to try to do a blemish-free fitting and piecing job.

If a wall is taller than 8 feet, order extra-long panels or allow for extra panels to piece out the height.

For board paneling or for more

Helpful Paneling Tools

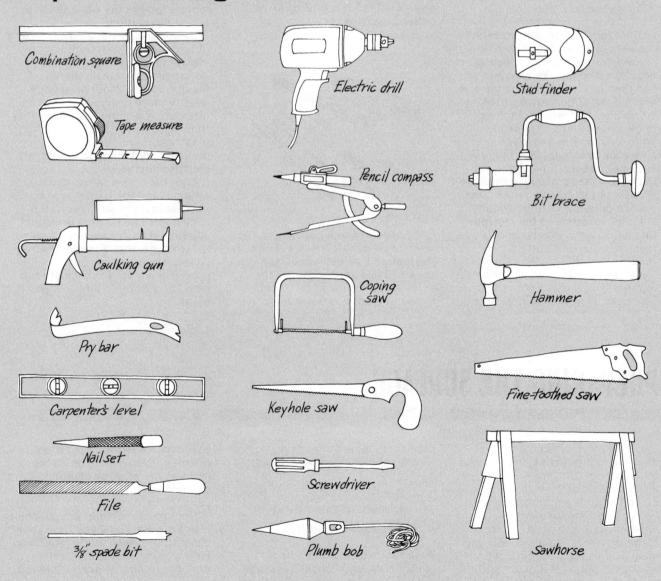

Combination square

Tape measure

Caulking gun

Pry bar

Carpenter's level

Nail set

File

3/8" spade bit

Electric drill

Pencil compass

Coping saw

Keyhole saw

Screwdriver

Plumb bob

Stud finder

Bit brace

Hammer

Fine-toothed saw

Sawhorse

complex installations, the job of estimating materials takes a bit more effort. Begin by measuring the wall or walls you plan to panel and duplicating them to scale on a piece of paper. Also draw windows, doors, and other large openings. Use a steel tape for measuring; consider using graph paper for the drawing (1 square can represent 1 foot).

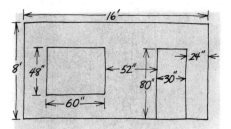

Figure the total wall area by multiplying its height times its width. From this amount, subtract the area of all openings.

Then, for solid board paneling, decide on the pattern of application (see pages 28-31) and the size and milling of boards you want.

Call a few dealers to get the best price for your type of paneling. When you've selected a dealer, take your square footage figures and sketches to him—he should have tables for computing the amount of material you need. Use his computation with the under-standing—written on the receipt—that all undamaged and uncut materials can be returned for refund or credit.

If any material must be special ordered, ask whether there is a service charge. Also inquire about

delivery charges for minimum orders.

If you will be using sheet paneling, ask the dealer whether or not you will need to back the material with gypsum wallboard for rigidity and fire protection. Building codes may require this, and if your dealer isn't thoroughly familiar with local codes, check with your building department.

Condition the paneling

All paneling should be stored in the room to be paneled for at least 2 days. This allows the paneling to become adapted to the room temperature and humidity, preventing warping or buckling after installation. You can stack paneling flat on the floor, sepa-rating each panel from the next by equivalent lengths of 2 by 4s or by furring strips.

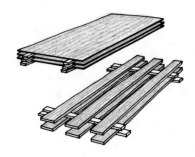

If you can't stack paneling in the room to be paneled, place it off the ground in a well-ventilated area that has approximately the same temperature as the room to be paneled.

It is essential to keep board paneling in a dry place; otherwise, it will absorb moisture, causing it to warp. If there's a danger of moisture, cover the boards with plastic or another nonporous material, making sure it fits loosely around the wood to allow for air circulation.

If a room to be paneled has a base of new plaster, wait until the plaster cures or apply a sealer before placing panels there. Plaster usually requires several days or more to cure, but you can often apply a primer sealer sooner than this. Panels left in a freshly plastered room absorb damaging moisture containing free lime, a caustic substance.

After the paneling has had a good airing, stand the panels side by side against the wall. Then step back and study how the grain and coloring of each panel blend with those of the next. Arrange the panels according to your prefer-ence. Then mark the back of each panel according to this arrange-ment.

PREPARING THE SURFACE

Paneling has this in common with painting, wallpapering, and most other interior finishing approaches: a successful outcome requires careful attention to the surface to be covered. The following section explains what you need to know about preparing a wall. It tells you about removing molding, locating studs, checking for flatness and

plumb, cleaning the surface, furring, shimming, and scribing.

Removing molding and baseboard

First, remove all old moldings, baseboards, and "shoes" (usually

cove-shaped strips on the base-boards). If you plan to reuse the molding material, be careful to prevent marring or splitting as you remove it.

Since most moldings are attached with finishing nails, you have your choice of two ways to remove them. First, you can gently hammer a thin, broad-bladed pry bar behind the molding and gently pry outward until that section of molding begins to give. Move the bar over a few inches and repeat the process until the entire piece comes loose. You'll find that some nails will stay with the molding and others will pull through and remain sticking out of the wall. Hammer in or pull those that remain.

A second way to remove molding is to locate the nails and, using a nailset or slim drift punch, drive each one all the way through the molding. After the molding is lifted off, enough of the nail protrudes so that it can be easily drawn out. For hardwood moldings found in some older houses, this method is the best.

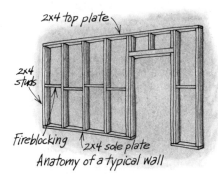

How to locate wall studs

Studs, which form the framework of a wall, are 2 by 4s standing vertically, normally spaced either 16 or 24 inches apart, center to center. Gypsum wallboard, plaster over another surface, or another wallcovering material usually conceals the studs in a frame wall.

Studs are nailed at the top and bottom of the wall frame to 2 by 4 horizontal "plates." At corners and around door and window frames, studs are usually doubled.

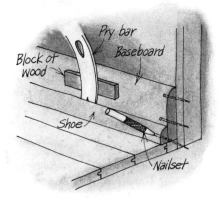

Anatomy of a typical wall

You'll have to locate the studs hidden within your present wall before you can install paneling. If furring strips are put on the wall (see pages 24 and 25 for installation tips) before panels are attached, the strips are nailed to the studs through the wall's surface. Or if paneling is installed on the wall without furring, panels are nailed directly to the studs through the wall.

Here are three methods for locating studs:

● Standard stud spacing is 16 or 24 inches from the center of one stud to the center of the next one. Measure from a corner to find and mark the first stud. Knock on the wall several times with your knuckles or the heel of your hand, listening closely. You will hear either a hollow sound or a solid thud. A thud means you have located a stud. A hollow sound means "Try again."

Knock and listen for solid sound

● A second method is to use a magnetic stud finder—an inexpensive little tool that operates by means of a magnetized needle that fluctuates when passed over a nail head. Of course, this won't work on

Search for nails using a magnetic stud finder

wall coverings attached with adhesive or where there is other metal beneath the wall's surface (plaster over wire mesh, for example).

● A third method is to probe into the wall, using a long nail or drill. If you find a stud, measure off 16 inches (or 24 inches) from that hole to find others. Because studs are not always as straight as they might be, it's a good idea to probe at several heights.

Probe for studs by drilling low holes

As you find each stud, mark it by snapping a chalk line (see page 66).

See that the surface is plumb, flat, and clean

If the surface is clean, flat, and plumb (see below), paneling can be applied with adhesives directly to the surface so long as there are subsurface wooden wall framing members (studs, plates, sills) to which it can be nailed.

First check the surface for flatness by holding a straight 2 by 4 against the wall. Check several places.

Then see if the wall is plumb. The easiest method is to hold a carpenter's level against the wall, checking to see if the level's bubble is framed properly between its hairlines. If you don't

have a level, you can tack a length of string with a weight on it (called a "plumb bob") to the ceiling in a corner; when it hangs still, measure the distance from the wall to the string at several points. A plumb wall will show no variations.

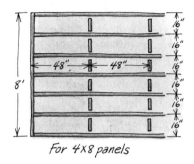

If the wall is flat and plumb, clean it with an ordinary household cleaner or a specialized wall cleaning product such as trisodium phosphate (TSP). Be sure to rinse the wall well and let it dry. Then use paneling adhesive to apply paneling directly to the surface.

If the wall is plumb but a little bumpy or damaged, use nails to apply paneling directly to it (without cleaning it).

Furring and shimming

Furring strips, usually 1 by 2s or 1 by 3s, are attached to a wall to provide a good nailing or gluing surface for paneling.

You will need to install a framework of furring strips in these cases:

1) If you are installing vertical solid board paneling.

2) If your wall is quite bumpy or severely damaged.

3) If your wall is significantly out of plumb.

4) If you need suitably spaced subsurface wall members for nailing.

5) If you want to install insulation under paneling.

Arrangement of furring strips depends upon the type of paneling

being applied and, in the case of board paneling, its direction. Three arrangements are shown below.

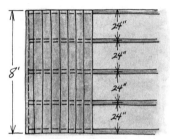

For 4 x 8 panels

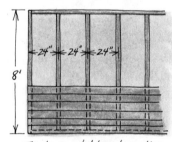

For vertical board paneling

For horizontal board paneling

Always be sure to apply strips securely. For wooden walls, nails should penetrate at least 1 inch into studs. For masonry walls, use concrete nails or expansion bolts.

Of course, furring strips should be plumb and offer a flat surface for attachment of panels. If the existing wall is severely out of plumb, it may be necessary to taper furring strips or to block them out slightly at one end.

For minute adjustments, use "shims." These are merely small wedges—usually shingles. When furring is in place, check for flatness using a long straightedge (a short one will not reveal

unevenness). Mark the portions of the furring that sag inward. These are the locations needing shims.

Simply tap them in place until the furring strips are flat and plumb; then just tack the shims to the wall so they won't fall out as you fasten paneling in place.

Shim out slight irregularities in flatness by driving shingles behind furring

Furring strips

If you're nailing directly to bare studs and they are more than 16 inches apart, you'll have to add 2 by 4 horizontal blocking between the studs to provide a nailing base for the edge of the paneling. Nail one block ¼ the distance down from the top plate, one block midway between floor and ceiling, and another block ¼ up from the bottom plate.

When you find that furring is necessary, remember that electric outlets, switchplates, and door and window frames will have to be adjusted to accommodate the increased wall thickness. Add your paneling's thickness to the furring's thickness and adjust electric outlets, switchplates, and door and window frames out that distance from their present positions.

This is not as difficult as it sounds. To adjust door and window frames, you simply add material of sufficient thickness to the existing framework to accommodate the depth of furring and paneling. Use good, dry lumber, taking care to match surfaces so that painting will cover the joint between old and new material. The illustration on page 26 shows a typical treatment for adjusting a window frame depth to match

How to Apply Furring Vertically

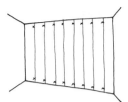

Step 1. *Find and mark locations of wall studs across the wall you intend to panel (see "How to locate wall studs," page 23).*

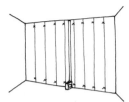

Step 2. *Measure height from floor to ceiling and cut furring strips the length of the wall's height minus 1 inch. Cut one furring strip for each stud.*

Step 3. *Allowing a ½-inch space at top and bottom, nail the top end of one furring strip to a stud at one end of the wall. Use 8d nails for nailing directly to studs, 10d nails for nailing through wallboard or other material into studs.*

Step 4. *Hold a carpenter's level against the side of the furring strip to check it for plumb; if necessary, move it until plumb, then nail it to the stud with a second nail, near the floor.*

Step 5. *Now use a level to check the front face for plumb and, by holding a long, straight 2 by 4 against it, check for flatness. Make any necessary adjustments by shimming the furring strip out from the wall.*

Step 6. *Install succeeding furring strips the same way, checking each one against the other for flatness. If necessary, shim out irregularities.*

How to Apply Furring Horizontally

Step 1. *Measure the wall from corner to corner. For an 8-foot-high wall, cut five furring strips the same length as the wall; for higher walls, add a furring strip for each additional 16 inches.*

Step 2. *At one of the wall's lower corners, tack one end of the first strip ½ inch up from the floor with one nail. Use 8d nails for nailing directly to studs, 10d nails for nailing through wall covering into studs. (See "How to locate wall studs," page 23.)*

Step 3. *Placing a carpenter's level on the opposite end of the furring strip, raise the strip until the air bubble in the level is centered. Then nail that end to a stud.*

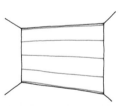

Step 4. *Finish nailing the furring strip to each stud between the two corners, one nail per stud.*

Step 5. *Check the furring strip for flatness by holding a long, straight 2 by 4 against it. If the furring strip dips anywhere, shim it out until it is flat.*

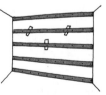

Step 6. *Install succeeding furring strips using the same methods. Check each one against the other for flatness. Shim out any irregularities.*

your new paneling. The same technique is used to prepare door frames.

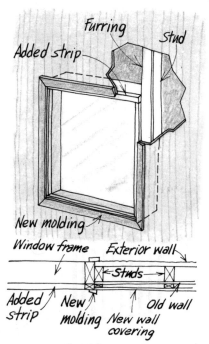

furring
Stud
Added strip
New molding
Window frame
Exterior wall
Studs
Added strip
New molding
New wall covering
Old wall

Electrical outlets and switch boxes are normally nailed to the side of a stud—usually toward the back. But sometimes they have a special flange by which they are nailed to the front of the stud. If this is the case, you'll have to cut away some wallboard or plaster to pry them loose. Older construction has metal boxes that will require some effort to pry loose, for the nails are driven at almost right angles. Newer construction has plastic boxes with slanted nail guides that make them easier to remove and reinstall. Caution: Turn off the current before you move electrical outlets.

A room is not as stable as it appears to be; its floor and ceiling shift as the house settles. If this future shifting is not taken into account when rigid wall coverings are installed, the result could be buckled walls. When you cut out vertical furring strips, allow for ½-inch space at top and bottom to prevent future settling of the room from popping out the panels. (Leaving ½-inch clearance between the bottom of a panel and the floor is another precaution many home builders observe.)

Paneling over plaster walls

You can easily install paneling over plaster walls by driving nails through panels and plaster into the studs.

Since plaster walls are usually found only in old houses, rarely will the wall be plumb or square at top and bottom. Because of this, it's recommended that panels be installed on furring strips. In the long run, placing furring is easier than sanding, patching, and sealing old plaster walls. And there's an added advantage: furring provides a "dead air" space behind the panels, enhancing both sound and thermal insulation properties.

Paneling over masonry walls

Masonry walls present a special problem. Because of moisture condensation, these walls should be waterproofed before you apply any covering to the surface.

If the concrete is new, it will also have a heavy alkali content. Alkalinity in concrete decreases with age—but not consistently. To be safe, ask your paint or masonry dealer to recommend a water-proofing masonry sealer that blocks alkali.

Use a cement grout to fill holes in concrete walls before sealing the surface. Spread it on smoothly and let it dry before applying the waterproofing sealer.

To further minimize the possibility of moisture penetrating the panels, use a vapor barrier paper or polyvinyl film between the concrete and the furring strips.

Attach furring to masonry, using expansion bolts.

If you're transforming a basement into a recreation room, you may want to create a basic framework of 2 by 4 studs to give enough depth for installing outlets and switches before you panel. In this case don't use furring strips; instead, place blocking between the studs to provide a nailing base.

UP GOES YOUR WALL PANELING

Once you've weathered the storms of wall preparation, you can breathe a sigh of relief, knowing the worst is over. Now comes the good part—the work that still requires careful attention to detail but yields the results you've been looking forward to since the moment you decided on paneling.

If you're installing sheet paneling . . .

Before you install the first panel, you'll want to make sure the first and last panels will be the same width. Do this by propping up all of the panels along the entire wall. If the last panel has to be much narrower than the first one, you'll want to cut both end panels to make them roughly equal in width. This is not so important when your paneling is simulated random-width boards.

Before actually cutting into any panel, though, study the following information about cutting panels and attaching with nails and adhesives. Also review the special considerations for paneling over plaster and masonry walls (see above) and for scribing (page 27).

Cutting panels

Before beginning to cut panels, check to see that ceiling height doesn't vary. (It may be irregular in older homes because of normal settling that occurs in all structures.) You need this information in order to allow a ½-inch clearance where paneling joins the ceiling so the panels won't buckle if the house settles.

Use a saw to cut wood and simulated-wood paneling materials. The blades should be for fine cutting—having 10 to 15 teeth per blade inch. On power circular saws, both portable and bench models, use plywood-cutting blades.

Cut panels face up if you use a handsaw or table saw; face down with a portable circular or saber saw.

As a precaution against splintering the panel edges or tearing the veneer, apply a strip of masking tape along the face of the cutting line. Be careful when removing the masking tape; its sticky side may be strong enough to splinter the wood.

When using a handsaw, start the cut at the panel's edge, holding the saw edge nearly flat to the surface in order to score the panel. Use

forward strokes only. If you find that keeping the saw on a straight line is a problem, clamp a straight board along the cutting line for the saw to ride against.

As you start to cut the panel, raise the saw to a 60° angle and—this is important—support the cut end when it begins to sag. Most paneling is very thin, and the vibration of the saw can easily snap a panel if it isn't firmly supported.

If you don't have someone to hold the sawed end for you, lay the panel across a couple of sawhorses (or their equivalent) with several furring strips or 2 by 4s

thrown across the horses for extra support.

Sawhorse

Scribing paneling. The first piece of paneling that you fit into the corner spot of a wall will probably not fit exactly the contours of the adjoining wall or floor. Nor is it likely to be level or plumb. To overcome this you must duplicate the irregularities of the adjoining surface on the paneling's edge. An inexpensive scribing tool is made especially for this purpose. It is shaped like a short compass: one leg has a pointed shaft while the other has a pencil (or you can use a compass).

Prop the panel into place about an inch from the uneven adjoining surface, using shingles if necessary to shim the panel into level or plumb. Holding the scribing tool's points parallel to each other, draw the scribe along the surface so that the pencil leg duplicates the unevenness onto the paneling.

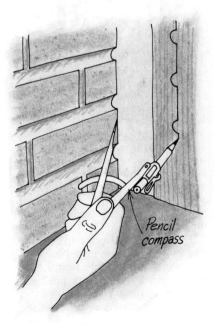

Pencil compass

Cutting out doors, windows, electric outlets, other openings. Doing this calls for paneling to be carefully cut to fit around them. Be sure to remove faceplates from switches and outlets. Measure from the nearest panel edge or corner to the edge of the opening or outlet; then measure to the opening's opposite edge. Measure also from the floor to the opening's bottom edge and again to the top edge. Transfer these measurements to the back of the panel, making certain you are measuring from the correct edge of the panel as it will be installed.

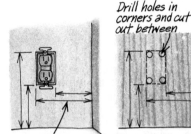

Drill holes in corners and cut out between

Measure placement of outlets and transfer to panels

Another way to mark the panels for cutting is to make a template from the protective sheets that come with many manufactured panels.

Because these sheets are the same size as the panels, you can tape one to the wall as though it were a panel. Mark the size of the outlet on the taped-up sheet or cut it out with a razor blade. Lay the sheet on the back of the panel and, using it as a pattern, mark the panel section so that the cutout will match the wall opening when the panel is installed.

To make cutouts in panels for electric outlets, light switches, small windows, and other small openings, drill holes in the panel in each of the four corners of the outlet mark that you've made. Then, using a keyhole saw or a saber saw, cut out the outlet hole. Cut from the front side of the panel when using a keyhole saw, from the back side when using a saber saw.

Attaching sheet panels

When installing sheet paneling, keep in mind one important fact: all edges must be supported.

(Continued on next page)

. . . Continued from page 27

This is no problem when you are applying panels directly to a wall. Nor is it a problem when you apply panels to a framework of studs or furring strips spaced regularly at 16 or 24 inches, center to center—you join the panels along the center of each framing member. But in any other case, you may have to use additional framing, as explained in the section on furring, page 24.

Nailing and fastening with adhesives are the two basic methods for applying most sheet panelings. Adhesives are the favorite method—fast and clean, and they don't subject panels to hammer dents.

Here's a brief rundown on how to use nails and adhesives:

Nailing. When nailing panels, be careful not to mar the surfaces. Also try to keep nails as inconspicuous as possible. Do this either by using nails that are color-matched to your paneling or by using finishing nails. Drive them into heavily textured areas or grooves, where they'll be least noticeable. For lapped panels, drive nails through flanges.

If the visible nail heads are objectionable, recess them, using a nailset, and then blend them to the surface, using a matched puttying or repair stick.

Use 1¼-inch nails for panels less than ½ inch thick; for ⅝ or ¾-inch panels, use 2-inch nails. Space them as shown in the illustration below.

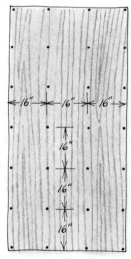

Proper nail placement for 4x8 panels

Adhesives. When applying panels with adhesives, follow manufacturer's package directions. Work one panel at a time—don't apply adhesive beyond the area that one panel will cover.

Here is the typical procedure: on furring or exposed wall framing, apply adhesive to the framing in squiggly stripes; for direct-to-wall applications, apply in uniformly spaced stripes 12 to 16 inches apart.

Drive four 1¼-inch finishing nails through the top end of the panel. Position it; drive nails part way into the wall to act as hinge pins. Pull the panel's bottom edge about 6 inches out from the wall and push a block behind it to hold it there; wait for the

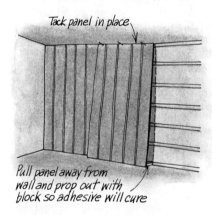

Tack panel in place.

Pull panel away from wall and prop out with block so adhesive will cure

adhesive to get tacky—8 to 10 minutes.

Next, remove the block and firmly press the panel into place. Force the adhesive into tight contact by knocking on the panel with a rubber mallet or hammering against a padded block. Don't mar the surface.

Drive the hinge-pin nails all the way in and nail the panel to the wall along the top and bottom edges, where nail heads will be covered by molding. All thin paneling materials require either

gluing or nailing within ½ inch of panel edges to prevent the panels from curling.

If you're installing solid board paneling

You measure, mark, and cut solid board panels the same way you do sheet paneling (see "Cutting panels," page 26), but because of their smaller size, the boards are easier to handle than the 4 by 8-foot sheets.

To prevent splintering, finished boards should be kept face up if you cut them with a handsaw or a table saw, face down if cut with a portable circular or saber saw.

As with sheet paneling, the two methods of application are nailing and use of paneling adhesive. For nailing, use finishing nails and recess the heads ¹⁄₃₂ inch below the surface, using a nailset. Disguise them by covering with color-matched puttying sticks.

Where you nail will depend upon the paneling's milling. Typical methods are shown below.

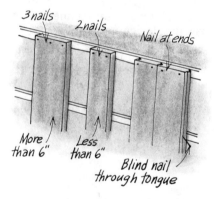

3 nails *2 nails* *Nail at ends*

More than 6" *Less than 6"* *Blind nail through tongue*

Apply adhesives as described for sheet paneling (at left), following manufacturer's directions. Also nail the two ends of each board, as shown in the illustration above.

Installing solid boards in various patterns

Here are some tips to keep in mind for installing solid board paneling in some of the most popular patterns:

Vertical pattern. Before paneling vertically with solid boards, you

Vertical

must attach horizontal furring strips (see pages 24-25). Then you should measure the board widths, measure the wall's length, and figure out how wide (or narrow) the final board will be. To avoid a sliver-size board, either split the difference so the first and last boards are the same size or take a little bit off of several boards so a full-size one will fit in the last spot.

When you put the first board into place against a corner, check the outer edge with a carpenter's

Check first board for plumb

level. If the board is not straight, mark it by scribing (see "Scribing paneling," page 27). Then trim it, using a plane or saw.

Attach the first board to the wall; then butt the second board against its edge and check for plumb before you nail or glue it to the wall. Do the same with all subsequent boards.

TIP FROM THE PROS

After installing solid board paneling across a wall, you may have trouble fitting the final board. To make this last board fit easily into place, cut its edges at a slight angle (about 5°) toward the board's back side.

Horizontal pattern. This doesn't usually require furring unless the wall is badly damaged and cannot be repaired. You can nail the

Horizontal

boards directly to the studs through the wall covering. So you don't end up with a very narrow board at the ceiling, work out and adjust its size as described under "Vertical pattern" (at left).

Start at one bottom corner of the wall and work up to the ceiling. Nail the first board temporarily at one end, ½ inch up from the floor. Then level the board and complete nailing. Using the same

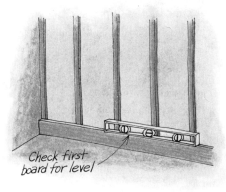

Check first board for level

methods, attach each additional board.

Diagonal pattern. Installed correctly this pattern appears to run from one wall onto the next. For this reason, cutting the board ends requires special attention. Boards are

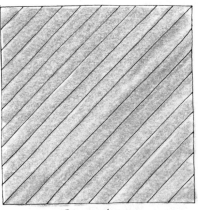

Diagonal

usually installed at a 45° angle unless the room's shape or style suggests an alternative. Furring isn't needed unless the wall is badly damaged.

Because you make all end cuts at 45°, you'll need a combination square with a 45° angle if you must use a handsaw. Otherwise, a

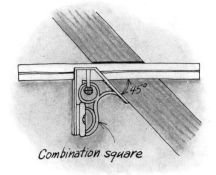

Combination square

table (bench) saw or radial-arm saw will do it all very accurately with one adjustment.

Where you begin the installation depends upon the direction in which you want the boards to run. Starting at the ceiling, the alternatives are either to the right or left. If you start at the bottom and want the pattern to run to the right, install the first board in the lower left corner. If the pattern runs to the left, start in the lower right corner.

(Continued on next page)

. . . Continued from page 29

Starting at one corner, measure the wall height from floor to ceiling. Measure the same distance across the bottom of the wall and make a mark. Establish a plumb line (see page 24) directly above this mark. Use a straight board to draw a line from the bottom corner to the top of the plumb line. This line should form a 45° angle.

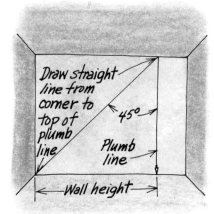

Measure the length of this line and transfer that measurement to a length of board paneling. Use a combination square to mark 45° end cuts. Then cut that board and

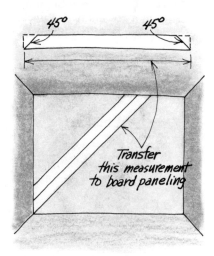

nail or glue it into place (see page 28). For each additional board, measure, mark, cut, and attach, using the same methods.

Herringbone pattern. Cutting the wood for this pattern requires even more care than cutting the wood for the diagonal pattern. And you may have to sand the cut ends lightly to make smooth joints.

As with a diagonal pattern, end cuts are usually made at a 45° angle.

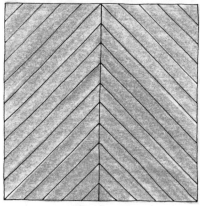

Herringbone

To install herringbone pattern, simply measure the width of your wall, dividing it into two equal areas according to the length of the wall and how many herringbones you want. Then board over each section according to instructions under "Diagonal pattern" (see page 29). Furring isn't necessary because boards stretch across plates and studs and can be nailed directly to them.

The herringbone pattern is a little trickier to handle as a first-time effort, but the final effect is well worth it. As with most paneling jobs, you start in one corner and work across the wall. You'll probably also encounter the usual out-of-plumb condition at your starting corner. In order for your final herringbone pattern to have the required symmetry, you may want to use the following procedure:

1) Decide how many herringbones will make a pleasing pattern for the expanse of wall you want paneled. Make sure that the center of each falls on a stud.

2) Using a plumb line, bisect the herringbones and mark the top and bottom of the wall. Take a straightedge and mark the wall or snap a chalk line (see page 66). These lines should fall over stud centers.

3) Temporarily nail a 1 by 2 guide strip along the first line and flush with it. This strip provides a steady "third hand" as you lay up the first floor-to-ceiling half of a herringbone.

4) As you put each piece in place, rest one edge against the guide strip. This allows you to maintain plumb as you work upward.

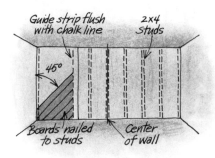

5) Once a plumb half-herringbone has been established, the guide strip can be removed, for the completed half-herringbone will serve as a plumb guide for the rest of the job.

Random width and thickness pattern. Here is a new approach to board paneling. You can install boards of different widths and

Random width and thickness

thicknesses by nailing them against horizontal furring or by attaching them (usually with adhesives) to 4 by 8-foot sheets of inexpensive plywood that are initially nailed to the studs. The wood used can be pieces of scrap lumber, arranged in any pattern you wish. The surface can be left natural or finished with paint, primer, stain, or sealer.

Board and batten pattern. You can install this pattern either vertically or horizontally according to directions given under those headings (pages 28-29). For the vertical pattern, you must first put up furring.

Square-edge boards are the best choice for this pattern—tongue-

and-groove or shiplap are unnecessary expenses.

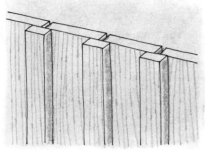

Board and batten

After you've installed the boards exactly as you would for vertical or horizontal paneling, simply nail a batten (a 1 by 2-inch wood strip) over the seam where the boards come together.

Board on gap pattern. You install this pattern in the same way as you do vertical or horizontal patterns. Each board is rabbeted—shiplap-style—usually 1 inch at one side and ¼ inch at the opposite side. When several boards

Board on gap

are butted together, you can see ¾-inch grooves between them.

Board on board pattern. Installation is the same as that for board and batten. Furring is necessary for

Board on board

vertical application. To save lumber, boards are spaced several inches apart. An outer board is nailed over this space.

Strip facing pattern. This is usually a vertical installation having solid boards of optional widths separated by ¾-inch strips of 1 by 2 batten laid on edge. Horizontal furring is required underneath. Install it

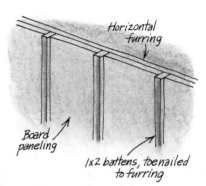

Horizontal furring

Board paneling

1x2 battens, toenailed to furring

using the same methods as those for vertical paneling (page 28) only attach the 1 by 2 battens sideways so that the 1-inch width faces away from the wall. Toenail the batten at each furring strip (see illustration above).

ADDING THE FINISHING TOUCHES

When all your panels are in place, all that remains is to add those small but important finishing touches.

You may want to add molding to these areas; the wall-ceiling joining line, the wall-floor joining line, and the edgings next to doors and windows.

Some—but not all—wall paneling needs to be sealed with a preservative, and some will need follow-up maintenance.

Moldings—they cover mistakes

In the boat-building trade, there's an old expression, "Putty and paint will make it what it ain't." In paneling, the expression is, "Moldings minimize mistakes."

Decorative moldings give a smooth finish to your paneling by covering rough edges. Moldings cover paneling edges at ceilings, corners inside and outside, and door and window frames. They also act as door stops, baseboards, shoes (strips that protect baseboards), and caps for wainscoting.

The range of possible moldings is wide. You can buy them at a lumberyard in standard designs of milled wood, wood-grain-printed plastic, vinyl, or aluminum. Most lumberyards carry a wide variety of molding strips to match whatever style of paneling you choose. Typical patterns are at right.

You can use ordinary 1 by 2 battens as moldings and 1 by 4 boards for baseboards, or—if you are a skilled craftsman—you may want to make your own moldings.

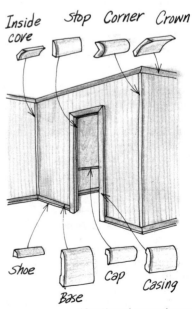

Inside cove   Stop   Corner   Crown

Shoe   Base   Cap   Casing

(Continued on next page)

Tools for Installing Moldings

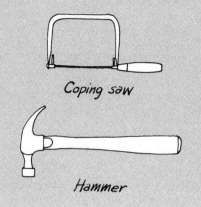

Miter box

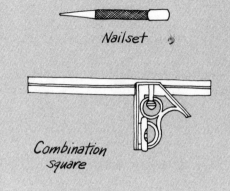

Coping saw

Nailset

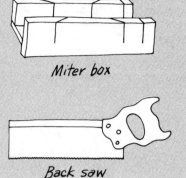

Back saw

Hammer

Combination square

. . . Continued from page 31

Illustrated above are the tools you'll need for installing moldings.

Measuring for molding. When measuring for molding—to frame a window, for example—measure the inside dimension (see illustration below) and cut your material accordingly. Bear in mind that

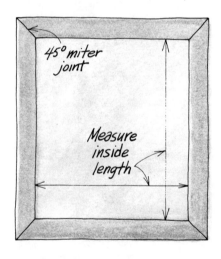

45° miter joint

Measure inside length

you must reverse the cuts on the ends of each piece of molding. Doing this sounds simple, but you will only have to make the mistake once to see why the statement is included here.

Reverse 45° cuts on ends

Cutting molding. Use the 45° angle on a combination square for marking miters (see "Mitering," page 19). Then, for cutting straight

lines and miters accurately, use a miter box (you can get an inexpensive miter box like the one shown above for about $5).

Curved, three-dimensional moldings, such as crown and base moldings, must be mitered and then cut to the proper curvature; use a coping saw to do this (see illustration).

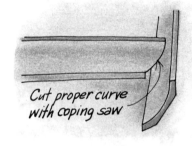

Cut proper curve with coping saw

Some professionals undercut the material when they are using thick molding. This allows the outer (visible) edge of the molding to fit tightly. Material on the underside of the cut is removed with a knife or rasp.

Especially when it's curved, coved, or fancy material, molding can be difficult to cut. Arrange to clamp the section you are working with, but be careful to pad the material in order not to mar it. As in any other type of woodwork, remember that a saw blade has thickness and allow for it, especially when sawing to the accuracies required with molding. The reason for clamping your material is that it tends to "creep" as the saw bites into it.

Fastening molding. Two methods are used for nailing moldings into

place: nailing with finishing nails, then recessing the heads with a nailset; and blind nailing. To blind nail, use a small knife or gouge to raise a sliver of wood that's large enough to hide the head of a finishing nail. (Don't break the sliver completely from the molding or you may not be able to replace it in its natural position.) After pulling the sliver to the side, nail into the cavity with a finishing nail and then glue the sliver back into place. You can tape the sliver down with a piece of masking tape until the glue is dry. Rubbing the spot lightly with fine sandpaper will remove all signs of fastening.

Rather than going through this entire procedure for one nail at a time, do it one step at a time, making all the gouges first and then recessing all the nails.

Finishes and maintenance

Normal wear and tear in a home may leave walls with a deposit of dirt and grease that, if not regularly cleaned off, can gradually change the color of wall paneling. For this reason it's a good idea to apply a washable finish.

You can do this on unfinished wood walls by applying a penetrating stain or varnish. For more about these finishes and how to apply them, see the following section on painting.

Finished walls—either vinyl-covered sheet paneling or solid board paneling—should be waxed when first installed and then cleaned and rewaxed about twice a year.

Mirrors—a Touch of Elegance

Covering a wall surface with mirrors lends a look of elegance to a room, frequently giving an effect of spaciousness you can get no other way. By reflecting light and the images of surrounding walls, ceiling, and furnishings, mirrors can brighten a room and—visually—double its size.

The type of mirrors most easily installed by homeowners come in a 12-inch-square size, ⅛ inch thick. They are boxed and sold by the dozen. These mirror squares are available from home improvement centers and hardware stores, as well as from glass dealers, in both plain and decorative (usually gold-veined or smoky) finishes. Decorative squares are more expensive than plain ones.

In each box of mirror squares, you'll find a sheet of small, double-edged tape squares used for installing the mirrors. Peel tape squares off this sheet and press one about 1 inch inside each corner of a mirror square. Then remove the covering paper on each tape square and press the mirror to the wall. But be sure to position mirror squares carefully—once they adhere to the wall, they are difficult to remove. If you have to remove a misplaced square, insert a straightedge under the square near each piece of tape and gently pry up.

To cut mirror tiles, you'll need a crayon or grease pencil, a straightedge, and a glass cutter (available from a glass dealer or at a hardware store). Straight cuts are easy to make, but don't try to remove less than 2 inches because the glass may break unevenly; have these narrow cuts made by a professional glass cutter.

Using the crayon, mark the two edges of the glass where you want to make the cut. Hold the straight-edge firmly against the glass, between the two marks. Then, squeezing the glass cutter firmly between your second finger and thumb, draw the cutting wheel across the surface of the glass, guiding it against the straightedge and pressing just hard enough to score the glass. Do this only once per cut.

Then place the mirror tile on a table so that the scored cutting line is directly above the table's edge. Hold the largest section against the table top and, with the other hand, firmly grasp the tile on the other side of the cutting line and snap downward. If the tile was properly scored, the break should be clean.

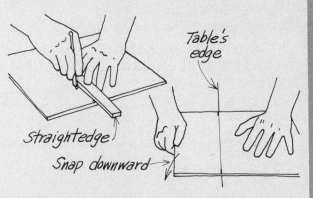

Straightedge

Table's edge

Snap downward

A word about installing regular mirrors: Regular mirrors are generally thicker, larger, and therefore considerably heavier than mirror tiles, and certainly more expensive. For these reasons, it is best to consult a professional glazier before you decide to use them.

Mirror tiles *are placed on wall surface; adhesive backing holds them securely.*

Color coordinate as you go

Rainbow-hued paint chips are compared with wallpaper samples before paint selection is made.

Paint as a graphic element

White and lavender paint contrast dramatically in contemporary living room (below). Colors extend into hallway (right), visually tying two rooms together. Interior design: Donald Wm. MacDonald, AIA.

PAINTING

Painting isn't nearly the chore it used to be. Whether you are forced to paint to cover someone else's decorating disaster or you merely want to change your decor, painting is still the fastest and easiest way to transform the visual impact of a room or entire house.

New paint materials feature the advantages of easier application, faster cleanup, and—most important—greater durability. Today's tools are less expensive and more versatile, making the job easier.

Prepare to discover a whole new world of do-it-yourself painting: a world of color variety, convenience-adding gadgetry, and imaginative decorating ideas. You'll find that it's almost impossible to go wrong.

This section will direct you in paint selection—introducing you to the awesome variety at your disposal. You'll find the illustrations of painting tools helpful. Within these pages are also instructions for surface preparation and painting sequence. Here, too, are hints for cleanup when the job is done.

If painting the four walls and ceiling of a room seems a bit overwhelming, you can get a real decorating boost by painting only one wall—choose a color that complements the color of the other walls and ceiling. And don't overlook the powerful new use of paint in creating supergraphics (see page 6).

The following chapter focuses on *interior* painting, but a special section at its close (pages 52-53) treats *exterior* painting.

CHOOSING THE RIGHT PAINT FOR THE JOB

Paint—from the simplest white-wash on primitive walls to the most modern, expensive enamel or latex—has been, and probably still is, the world's most popular wall coating. Why? Because it's colorful, it's easy to apply and maintain, and it permits quick redecoration as mood or fashion dictates.

Latex, enamel, varnish, and polyurethane are a sometimes confusing grab bag of names for a painter to grapple with. Recently developed paints are easily applied, quick to clean up, and, most important, long lasting. Improvements are continually reaching the stores. Ask a paint dealer about new products. In addition to helping you choose the right paint for the job, he'll know of the latest developments in the field.

TIP FROM THE PROS

You'll want to develop the knack of picking the right color for the right room. Doing this will help make a cold room seem warmer, a small room seem larger, and an uninviting room seem more friendly.

Basically, dark colors make walls appear to close in; light colors, in contrast, seem to expand walls. The way to make a room look its largest is to paint it white, off-white, or antique white.

Choose warm and light colors (reds, oranges, yellows) in sun-shy north and east-facing rooms. These colors will also help to make a low ceiling seem higher. On the other hand, cooler, darker colors (violets, blues, greens) are appropriate for sunny south and west-facing rooms. Dark colors are especially effective in making a high ceiling seem lower.

Because paint comes in a profusion of brand names and grades, selecting one of good quality can be confusing. Your best bet is to use price as a guide—a good quality paint may cost nearly twice as much as the cheapest paint available. But if you use a cheap paint, you may have to apply more initial coats and re-paint more frequently.

Each paint family has a different quality and a special use. Your basic choice is between an oil-base (alkyd) or a water-base (latex) product; they are explained below. The two groupings that follow oil and water-base paints are for special painting situations.

Oil-base paints (alkyds)— the work horses

For a long time the champions of the market, oil-base paints are known for their good qualities. Their washability and durability remain better than those of latex paints. They generally level out better, drying free of brush marks. And they have "bite," a sticking quality not always found in latex.

Available alkyd finishes are flat, satin, semigloss, or gloss (the higher the gloss, the smoother the finish and the greater the wash-ability and durability). Alkyds are paints for places most susceptible to dirt and wear—the kitchen and bathroom, or woodwork anywhere.

Most modern alkyds don't require thinning; stirring will bring the paint to the proper consistency. It takes only paint thinner to clean up afterwards.

A special type of alkyd—interior-exterior, quick-drying enamel—has a brilliant, tilelike finish that is extremely durable. An added quality is its high resistance to odor and dirt, making it a prime candidate for applying to kitchen and bathroom cabinets and wardrobe and closet doors.

Many newly developed enamels —such as synthetic enamel—are also available, all with excellent washability and color retention; they range in sheen from high to very low. They're used for the same

purposes as the standard oil-base paints.

Latex paints— the smoothies

Because latex paints are easy to use (latex enamel can be an exception, depending on your skill with a brush), quick drying, and nontoxic, they have surpassed alkyds as the most popular paints. Other pluses: they are smooth-spreading and relatively odorless, and they can be applied to damp surfaces. Simple tool cleanup with soap and warm water and easy touch-up add to the advantages.

Latex finishes range from flat to semigloss. You can apply latex to nearly all surfaces (exceptions would include acoustical ceilings, which take a special paint, or tile surfaces, to which epoxy paint adheres best—see page 38).

Flat vinyl, a specially made latex, leaves a dull finish that is washable and alkali resistant. Surfaces covered best by flat vinyl include block, masonite, and fiberboard.

For surfaces where durability and washability are desired and you prefer to work with a latex, use a semigloss enamel. It is washable and durable and can be used in the kitchen, bathroom, and laundry. It goes on smoothly but does not level as well as alkyds and tends to show brush marks.

Wood stains—to enhance the grain with color

Many types of stains are available— each one made for a particular wood, effect, or condition. It's best to discuss the job with your paint dealer before choosing a stain.

One interior stain is in such general use and is so easy to apply that it deserves mention—it is pigmented or dye-colored wiping stain. You simply brush it on, wait awhile, then wipe it off. Its typical uses are for such wood surfaces as walls (particularly solid-board paneling),

Painting Terms You Should Know

Acrylic. One of the resins in latex paints used to bind other ingredients.

Alkyd. A common term for oil-base paints; cleanup and thinning are done with solvent.

Caulking compound. A semidrying or slow-drying plastic material used to seal joints or fill crevices around windows, chimneys, and the like. It usually is applied with a caulking gun or with a putty knife.

Enamel. A finishing material with very fine pigments; provides a smooth, hard finish, either glossy or semiglossy.

Epoxy. A common name applied to an exceptionally durable, plasticlike paint.

Gloss. The shininess or lack of shininess of a paint finish. Paint finishes described as "glossy" have the highest luster; those described as "flat" have little luster; "semigloss" has a medium luster.

Latex paints. Water-base paints, sometimes called "vinyl" or "acrylic" paints; cleanup and thinning are done with soap and warm water.

Masking. Protecting—usually with tape and/or sheets of paper—any area you do not want painted.

Oil-base paints. Paints with resins and other ingredients made of various oils; cleanup and thinning are done with solvent.

Polyurethane. A resin. Also the common name applied to the clear plastic coating material made from this resin.

Primer. A first coat—usually a special paint—applied to help a finish coat adhere to the surface; may be latex or oil-base.

Shellac. A coating made with a resinous material called "lac"; popularly used as a clear sealer or finish.

Stippling. Applying paint by tapping the tip of a brush against a surface, creating a textured effect.

Thinners/Solvents. Volatile liquids used to regulate the consistency of paint and other finishes; also for cleanup when using oil-base paints.

Trisodium phosphate (TSP). A strong cleaning agent sold in solution under various brand names and available in powder form under the name of TSP.

Varnish. A liquid coating that converts to a translucent or transparent solid film after application.

Vinyl. The name of a class of resins. Vinyl acetate is commonly used in latex paints. Polyvinyl chloride is used in some solvent-thinned coatings in which high chemical resistance is called for. Many other vinyl derivatives appear in various specialized coatings.

Water-base paints. (See "Latex paints")

---

cabinets, and trim. Wood tone colors are available in a wide range. Cleanup requires paint thinner.

Polyurethane, varnish, and shellac—the shiny set

Though sometimes pigmented, these are generally clear finishes. They're commonly used to cover bare or stained wood surfaces when you want the grain to show through.

Polyurethanes

These plastic coatings are applied to cabinets and wood paneling where extreme durability and washability are required. Available in both clear and colored finishes, they are easy to use. Polyurethane interior satin finish is a popular choice because neither scuffing, water, nor grease will harm the surface. One type of polyurethane—penetrating resin sealer—soaks into the wood rather than coating the surface. This is the type to use where you want to maintain the

Wood grain *shows through clear polyurethane coating; finish is durable, washable.*

wood's texture. Use paint thinner for thinning and cleanup.

Varnishes

Resin-based coatings, varnishes have many of the same uses as polyurethanes. Finishes range from low sheen through satin sheen and semigloss to high gloss. Toughness is a prime characteristic: varnishes are resistant to marring, abrasion, and water stains. Many types of varnishes are available—ask your paint dealer for recommendations. Use paint thinner for thinning and cleanup.

Shellac

Because it allows the wood grain to show through, shellac can be used for finishing wood paneling, cabinets, doors, and trim. Its finish is glossy and its color is either natural amber (orange) or clear (white). Shellac dries quickly (30 minutes). One disadvantage is that it leaves brush marks, requiring a top coat of varnish to cover the marks. Another is that shellac is damaged by water, making it unsuitable for use in bathrooms, kitchens, laundry rooms, and other areas exposed to moisture. Use "shellac thinner grade" alcohol for thinning and cleanup.

Special paints—the problem solvers

Many homes have surfaces that require special finishes. Such surfaces include acoustical ceilings, nonporous surfaces like tile, and walls with imperfections. For these, special paints are available.

● Acoustical ceiling paint. Acoustical ceilings lose some of their sound-deadening qualities when covered with ordinary paint. Acoustical ceiling paint is a porous, flat paint that does not change the panels' acoustics. It comes in only a few colors and is usually applied with a sprayer, but a special roller can be used.

Acoustical ceiling paint can also be applied to simulated acoustical surfaces, perforated acoustical tile, and mineral tile. It dries quickly to a flat finish. Thinning is done with water; cleanup is with soap and warm water.

Acoustical ceiling paint *rolls on easily; does not change panels' acoustics.*

● Epoxy paint. For hard, nonporous surfaces (including ceramic and metal tile, plastics and plastic laminate, porcelain, fiberglass,

and glass) epoxy is the best (and sometimes the only) paint to use. It is usually found in semigloss or high gloss and comes in a wide range of colors.

Epoxy is extremely durable, withstands scrubbing, and resists abrasion. The most effective epoxies come in two cans that are mixed together just before you begin the job. One disadvantage of epoxy paint is that it is very fast drying, making it difficult to apply without brush marks. Another is the difficulty of cleanup; you must use a special epoxy thinner immediately upon finishing the job.
● Textured paint. These include basic texture paint, sand paint, and stipple enamel. Such paints are thick substances containing texturizers. They have recently gained in popularity both because they effectively disguise wall imperfections and because their general esthetic effect is pleasing. They are available in white and pastels.

You add a basic texture paint to a flat wall paint; use a brush to apply it to a small area. Then, while the paint is still wet, you create a rough finish with a trowel, putty knife, whisk broom, brush, sponge, paint roller, or other implement—even with a piece of crumpled paper.

Add texture *by running carpet-type roller over freshly painted surface.*

Sand paint is a latex to which you add 30-mesh sand or sandlike material. When applied with a brush or roller, it produces a coarse, sandpaperlike finish, making it a popular covering for gypsum wallboard that has taped joints.

Stipple enamel also produces a textured effect—very much like the skin of an orange. It's available in

various degrees of texture and in low and high gloss. Applied with a brush or roller first, stipple enamel is given its final texture with a carpet-type roller.

Surface/Finish Chart

Surface	Latex flat	Latex semigloss	Oil-base flat	Oil-base semigloss	Oil-base gloss enamel	Varnish	Shellac	Polyurethane
Dry walls, ceilings	●	●	●	●	●		●	
Plaster walls, ceilings	●	●	●	●	●			
Wood paneling			●	●	●	●	●	●
Kitchen and bathroom walls		●		●	●			
Wood trim		●	●	●	●	●	●	●
Window sills		●			●	●		●
Acoustical ceiling (Also see "Special paints: the problem solvers")	●							
Wood cabinets, shelves			●	●	●	●		●

How much paint will you need?

You can take advantage of your paint dealer's experience by allowing him to estimate the quantity of paint you'll need for the areas to be covered. To do this, you'll need to provide him with the square footage of the surfaces to be painted.

Determine the square footage of wall area you will paint by measuring the distance around the room and multiplying this figure by the room's height. Then estimate how much of this area contains surfaces that won't be painted— fireplaces, windows, wallpapered surfaces, and woodwork that will be painted separately. If these surfaces represent more than 10 percent of the room, deduct this amount from the total wall area.

Figure the ceiling area by multiplying its width by its length. Roughly estimate the area of cabinets, doors, and other relatively small surfaces.

SELECTING & USING PAINTING TOOLS

Though choosing the right type and quality of paint is important, it alone can't guarantee the success of a finished paint job. Even the best paint, if applied improperly and with the wrong tools, can produce disappointing results. If you choose your tools wisely and learn how to handle them correctly, you'll save yourself time and money—and possibly a headache or two.

Tools you'll need

No matter how large or small the job, painting requires the correct paint applicators, preparation tools, and general supplies. Before you start to paint, carefully read the following section to make sure you have all the needed equipment (see illustrations of various tools on the next page).

Brush choice is important

Selecting the correct brushes is almost as important as selecting the paint. You must decide on the size of brush appropriate to the nature of the project and the type of bristle best suited to the paint you will use. And you should be able to recognize the difference between brushes of good and poor quality.

Natural bristles (hog hair). These brushes have been traditionally used to apply oil-base paints, varnishes, shellac, and polyurethane. Natural bristles are not suitable for applying latex paints because the bristles soak up the water in the paints, quickly becoming soggy and useless.

Synthetic bristles. These nylon or nylonlike bristles are best for applying water-base paints. However, some synthetic bristles look and work very much like natural bristles and can also effectively apply oil-base finishes. Ask your paint dealer about a special type of synthetic bristle brush that you can use for applying varnishes and shellac—two finishes that would ruin an ordinary synthetic bristle.

What size brush? Having the right size brush can save you a lot of time and trouble. For painting trim and hard-to-reach places, a 1-inch brush does the job neatly. Window sashes, shutters, and edgings are best painted with a 1½ or 2-inch angular sash brush.

For woodwork, cabinets, doors, cupboards, shelves, beams, stair steps, and other medium-size surfaces, try a 2½ or 3-inch brush. For walls, ceilings, and most paneling, use a 3½ or 4-inch brush (you might prefer a roller for these larger areas; see next column).

Check for quality. Good quality brushes show a marked difference in performance from cheaper "economy" brushes. Follow the guidelines given below in selecting a quality brush.

Check for "flagging" of the bristles. ("Flags" are the split ends of bristles, and you need lots of these—more flags mean more paint is held on the bristles permitting smoother application.) Most of the bristles should be long, but check to make sure that some short bristles are mixed among the longer ones. Bristles should be

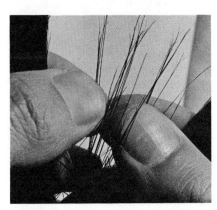

"Flagged" bristles *varying in length are characteristic of quality brushes.*

thick, flexible, and tapered so that they're thicker at the base than at the tip. And they should be set firmly into the handle. A brush should feel comfortable in your hand—not so awkward or heavy that using it will tire you.

It's especially wise to select a top-quality brush if you're planning

on extensive painting. But for small or occasional jobs, a less expensive brush might do.

A word of caution about buying "bargain" brushes. The chief problem with inexpensive brushes is their tendency to shed more "hair" than a cat, and no one wants a hairy paint job. A quality brush, properly used, will turn out quality work. There are many brushes of acceptable quality available. Choose yours in terms of the job you want to do and the length of time you feel you are going to need the brush. Your paint dealer has a wide range of brushes, priced from under $1 to over $30. Describe the job to him; he'll help you choose the proper brush.

Paint rollers and accessories

When you want to paint a large, flat area quickly and easily, a roller is your answer. With it, you'll need a few accessories.

Take giant steps with a roller. A good roller has a heavy-gauge wire frame, an expandable cage-type sleeve, a cover that fits over the sleeve, and a comfortable handle threaded to accommodate an extension pole for long reaches. A few different standard roller widths are available, but one size —9-inch—will handle nearly all interior paint jobs.

In selecting a roller, the roller cover is the most important consideration. The nap material of the cover is either nylon blend, lambskin, or mohair. The synthetic blend is recommended for use with latex, though it can be used with oil-base products. Lambskin covers are for applying oil-base paints only. Because it has a very short and fine nap, a mohair cover provides the smoothest finish for both alkyds and latex—particularly important to know when you want to apply enamel or varnish.

Nap thickness of roller covers varies from ¼ to 1¼ inch. Shorter napped covers are best suited for applying paint to smooth surfaces; medium naps handle textured surfaces; long naps are necessary for rough surfaces.

Regular-size rollers don't meet

Helpful Painting Tools

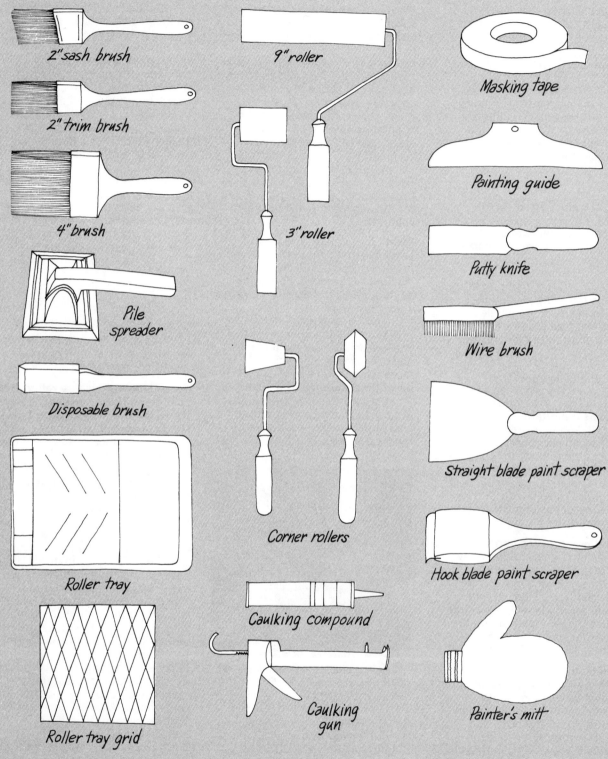

2" sash brush

2" trim brush

4" brush

Pile spreader

Disposable brush

Roller tray

Roller tray grid

9" roller

3" roller

Corner rollers

Caulking compound

Caulking gun

Masking tape

Painting guide

Putty knife

Wire brush

Straight blade paint scraper

Hook blade paint scraper

Painter's mitt

OTHER HELPFUL TOOLS: 1-inch brush, carpet roller cover, extension poles (2' and 4'), pan-type tray, sandpaper, liquid sanding agent, window scraper, wood putty, bucket, spackling compound, patching plaster, liquid paint remover, wall cleaner (TS P), stepladder, drop cloth, mixing paddle, wire brush-cleaning comb, paint thinner, plastic disposable gloves, paint can opener, wipe rags every painting need. That's why paint dealers offer these special rollers: a trim roller, 1 to 3 inches wide, for painting trim and sash; a corner roller with a beveled donut shape, for painting corners, ceiling borders, and paneling grooves; a carpet roller for stippling (see page 37); and an acoustical ceiling roller made of grooved foam.

Helpful accessories. Besides the roller, a handful of accessories will complete your set-up.

Roller trays—the most important accessories for roller painting— are available with either shallow or deep wells, suitable for small or large jobs. Most have corrugated slopes to allow excess paint to be squeezed off the roller. A plastic or metal grid placed over the slope will help separate any unusable residue of a thick paint. (This grid can also be placed inside a 5-gallon paint "drum"—ask your dealer—and hung from the rim. This eliminates the several refills that a tray would require.) Plastic disposable tray liners make cleanup quick and easy.

Extension poles to which rollers are attached allow you to reach high walls and ceilings without needing ladders or scaffolding. Three and 4-foot poles handle nearly all interior situations.

Other tools for applying paint

In addition to brushes and rollers, you may want to consider these helpful paint applicators.

Pile spreaders are popular because they are faster to use than a medium-size brush and more versatile than a roller—they can reach into corners. These handy gadgets have a nylon, mohair, or lambswool applicator surface, a foam middle layer, and a rigid backing, all replaceable and all fitted on a comfortable handle. Some have guides for neat, easy edgework. You can buy a special square pan-type paint tray for use with these spreaders (or simply use a roller tray).

Brushlike applicators are available that are totally disposable or have replaceable applicator pads. For small jobs or quick touchup, disposable spreaders may prove the most economical.

The painter's mitt is an old standby—a large, lambskin glove that is placed over a plastic glove on your hand and dipped into the paint. Being flexible, it's ideal for painting such irregular surfaces as pipes, grills, and radiators.

PREPARATION...NAIL HOLES TO DROP CLOTHS

Before you open even one can of paint, it's important to prepare the area for painting. This may involve moving furniture out of the way, protecting items that cannot be moved, repairing damaged surfaces, and cleaning surfaces so the paint will adhere.

Organizing a room for painting

Ideally, a room should be cleared of all furniture and accessories before painting begins. Practically, though, this is not always possible.

Move lightweight furniture— chairs, small tables, throw rugs, and so forth—into an adjoining room. Then push the heavy furniture to the center of the room and cover it with drop cloths.

Take down curtains and drapes (and all their fixtures, if you don't plan on painting them), along with all wall-mounted objects. Hooks and nails from which objects have been hung can remain in place during painting. But if you intend to rearrange, pull out hooks or nails and patch the holes (see the next page).

It is best to remove knobs, handles, and locks from doors, windows, and cabinets. Also, unscrew all switchplates and outlet plates. Place previously painted metal hardware and fixtures in a can filled with paint remover. This way, when you're finished painting, you'll have clean hardware and fixtures to reinstall.

Place anything you want painted the same color as the room on newspaper or a drop cloth and paint it before replacing it.

If your room has objects that can't be moved, protect them from spatters, spills, and possible slips of the brush in these ways:
● Place dropcloths over carpets, counters, and other heavy or permanent installations.
● Tie plastic bags around ceiling-hung fixtures and doorknobs and other fixtures you don't remove.
● Use masking tape to cover edges of window panes.

Preparing the surface to receive paint

Properly preparing the surface to be painted is a key factor in preventing possible cracking and peeling after the paint dries.

Stripping old paint

Sometimes the old finish is in such bad condition—extensive scaling and cracking—that the paint must be removed entirely. The easiest way to remove it is to use a commercial liquid paint remover. You might also try an electric paint softener. With either, the softened paint is scraped off with a straight blade scraper. The scraped surface is then lightly sanded clean and smooth.

Scraper
Electric paint softener

Removing wallpaper

Painting over wallpaper is possible, but it can be a risky business—the durability of your paint job will depend on the condition of the paper. It must be smooth and stuck tightly to the wall. Remove or re-paste loose pieces and puncture any air bubbles (see page 69). Then apply a sealing primer, such as pigmented shellac or flat oil-base enamel undercoat. When the sealer is thoroughly dry, cover with a liberal finish coat of an oil-base or latex paint.

The recommended procedure, though, is to remove the wallpaper, especially if it's tearing and flaking. Use a wallpaper steamer or one of the products made for soft-ening old wallpaper paste, both available from your paint or wall-paper dealer (see page 63). Make sure all the paste is removed and thoroughly wash the wall with a solution of trisodium phosphate (TSP) and water. Rinse well; allow the surface to dry for 24 hours.

For more helpful hints on remov-ing old wallpaper, see page 63.

Sandpapering

One of the final steps in surface preparation is sandpapering. The old finish requires light sanding if it is flaking lightly. Rough, bare wood needs sanding, as does a patched area. And when you plan to paint over a glossy paint surface, you must roughen the old finish so the new paint will adhere. On surfaces that have a very high sheen, start deglossing with a coarse sandpaper and finish with a fine grit paper. Greasy areas should be cleaned (see below) before sanding so that sanding will not work grease into the wood.

Dusting and washing

The last step of surface preparation is an overall dusting of the area and a thorough washing of the surfaces to be painted.

Begin by dusting everything. Make sure to wipe areas over windows, doors, and cabinets. A good vacuuming is also recom-mended. Be particularly thorough if you have done much sanding in the room.

Wash the areas you plan to paint with a mixture of trisodium phos-phate (TSP) and water. Scrub a

small area, rinse it well, and then move on. In the kitchen and bathroom, scrub vigorously and rinse thoroughly. For excessively greasy spots, first use a sponge soaked with paint thinner. Blot the thinner dry and wash with TSP. Rinse the surface well.

Woodwork also requires a wiping with TSP and rinsing to remove oily spots completely.

Allow about 24 hours for all washed areas to dry completely.

Repairing holes and other surface damage

Minor household repair is often required before painting. A new coat of paint may cover the surface at first, but if the surface hasn't been properly prepared, you'll be painting again in a short time.

Before you open that can of paint, inspect the area closely for small holes, light flaking, and other minor damage not readily apparent.

Patching small holes and cracks

Small holes and cracks require a minimum of time and materials to repair.

Nail holes can be filled with a tiny amount of wood putty or a ready-mixed spackling compound.

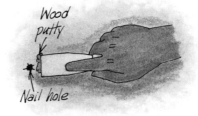

Small cracks and other small holes should be brushed clean and then filled with wood putty, spackling compound, or patching plaster. Be sure to dampen the surface (or better still, seal it with pigmented shellac; allow to dry) so that spackling compound or patching plaster will adhere. Apply each filler with a flexible, narrow-blade putty knife.

"Checking" is a term for a series of small cracks on wood surfaces (and in their finishes) caused by the expansion and contraction of the wood as it ages. Repairing these small cracks requires a little extra work. Sand the damaged

finish to bare wood. Apply a primer and allow it to dry thoroughly. Fill the wood cracks with wood putty, using a flexible knife. Again, apply a primer and allow it to dry.

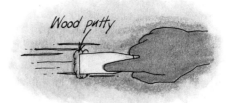

Sand all patched areas until smooth. If you are repainting with a light-colored paint, some patches may show through later as darker spots. To avoid this possibility, prime the patches with the same color paint you'll be using for the finish coat.

Patching large holes and cracks

Repairs of this kind require a little extra time, care, and carpentry skill.

Holes in plaster over lath. Here's the repair method to follow. Knock out all the loose plaster with a wire brush and screwdriver. Clean out the plaster in and behind the lath to provide a clean surface for the new plaster to adhere to. Brush the area clean and dampen it with a sponge for better adhesion. Force a layer of patching plaster between the lath strips.

If the hole is smaller than 4 inches square, fill it with one layer of patching compound; if the hole is larger than 4 inches square, fill it with three layers.

The first layer should include some patching plaster that fills in behind the lath. Work from the

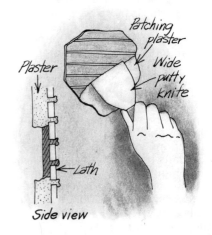

outer edges to the middle, filling about one-third the depth of the patch. Score the first layer with a nail. Allow to dry; redampen the

area. Apply a second layer to two-thirds the depth. Allow to dry; finish filling the hole. When the surface is dry, sand smooth and apply a primer or sealer.

Holes that have no backing. Use the following technique for holes 4 inches or less. Clean the hole. Cut a piece of hardware cloth (wire screening) to a size slightly larger than the hole. Tie one end of a wire to the center of

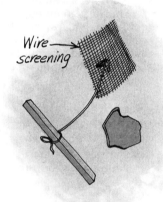

Wire screening

the screen; tie the other end to a 6-inch stick. Push the screen through the hole. Then draw the screen tightly to the back of the wall by rolling the wire up on the stick until the wire is taut.

Dampen the area. Fill the hole to half its thickness with patching plaster.
Allow the plaster to dry thoroughly. Cut the wire even with the

plaster and redampen the patch. Fill the hole flush with the wall. Allow it to dry; then sand it smooth. Apply a primer or sealer.

Large holes in gypsum wallboard. Here is a simple patching technique. Cut out a neat rectangle around the hole, using a sharp knife or hacksaw blade. Then cut a

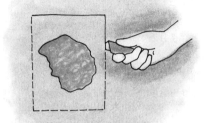

patch from another piece of gypsum wallboard, making it 1 inch wider on all four sides than the rectangle you've cut out of the wall.
Laying the cut piece of gypsum wallboard surface-side down, cut a plug the same size as the wall's rectangle without scoring the paper on the surface of the plug. Lift off the 1 inch of cut wallboard around the four sides of the patch from the front paper; this leaves a 1-inch margin of paper around all four sides of the gypsum patch.

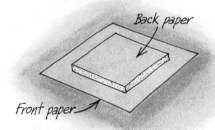

Back paper

Front paper

Spread a thin layer of spackling compound around and on the edges of the hole in the wall. Position the patch, pressing it into the hole until even with the wall surface.

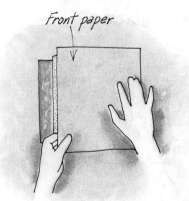

Front paper

Cover the seams and entire surface with spackle; allow this to dry before smoothing with sandpaper.

Large wall or ceiling cracks. These require special attention. Because of continuing structural expansion and contraction, cracks filled with such rigid materials as plaster and spackling compound can give continual trouble. The answer is a special patented crack patcher. It is a combination of a pliable coating material and an elastic bridging fabric. Because a crack patcher "gives" with further house movements, cracks don't reappear. To apply, follow the instructions given with the product.

Repairing joint separations

Occasionally an opening appears between different types of building materials, such as between a window frame and part of the wall surface. Hammer, nails, and caulking material come in handy for these common repairs. Minor gaps are easily sealed with caulking compound and a caulking gun.

Caulking gun

Other possible separations may be caused by loose molding and baseboard or slipping mitered joints. For tips on repairing, see the *Sunset* book *Basic Home Repairs.*

When the old paint gives out

Chalking, blistering, peeling, cracking, and flaking paint are all signs that the surface needs attention. Though these common problems usually occur on exterior surfaces, they occasionally happen with interior paint jobs as well.
Chalking is the decomposition of a paint film into a loose powder that appears on the film's surface. Heavy chalking, which leaves an unprotected surface, should be thoroughly brushed off before you repaint the surface.
Blistering and peeling are normally the result of paint having

been applied over a moist wood surface. If the surface is allowed to dry completely before painting, you probably won't have this problem. But sometimes moisture seeps into the wood after painting, regardless of how careful you are. It may come from a crack on the outside of the house or a leaky pipe inside the wall. To remedy this, locate and cut off the source of moisture. After repairing these surfaces, allow a 2-day drying period before repainting with a water-base paint (this will allow remaining moisture to escape through the surface without further peeling and blistering).

Mildew also causes paint to blister and peel. For remedies, see the next column.

Alligatoring (cracks resembling alligator skin), other cracking, and flaking are the result of a mistake made in applying paint. One mistake could have been applying a second coat of paint before the first had dried. Others may have been applying the paint too thickly or applying too many coats. Whatever the cause, here is the solution.

Remove all loose paint. A hook-blade scraper does a fast job on

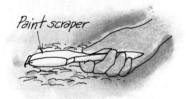

Paint scraper

large areas; straight blade scrapers are more convenient for small areas. And a wire brush can

handle any tiny flaking—use sandpaper to taper the edges. Sand all surfaces smooth and brush clean. (Cases of excessive damage call for complete paint removal; see page 41 for details about paint removal.)

Apply two coats of primer to repaired areas, allowing each coat to dry thoroughly. If you're not prepared to paint the entire wall surface, you have to apply one or more coats of the final finish to match the color and sheen of the old paint around these areas.

The problem of mildew

Mildew has already been mentioned as a cause of paint flaking when it develops beneath the paint surface. But mildew also gives a dingy, unclean look to the surface. Such sootiness is often mistaken for dirt, but dirt doesn't bleach out —mildew does. And though painting over mildew may slow its growth for a short time, the mildew will eventually show through and— goodbye, paint job.

Dark spots on painted ceiling, along edge of molding were caused by mildew; spores spread to papered wall, requiring removal of covering.

Even with mildew-control paint additives available, mildew must be eliminated before repainting. One effective method is to scrub the affected areas with a solution of 2/3 cup trisodium phosphate (TSP), 1/3 cup strong detergent, 1 quart bleach, and 3 quarts warm water. Another method is to use a concentrated liquid mildew eradicator that can be purchased from your paint dealer. Wearing gloves and protecting your eyes, apply either solution with a brush, scrubbing vigorously. Allow the solution to remain on the surface for a few minutes and then rinse well. Let the surface dry for 2 days.

Water damage

Sometimes moisture penetrates a wall, flaking and staining paint and rotting wood.

First, get rid of the source of moisture (repair leaking pipe or hole in roof or exterior wall). Cut out and replace any rotted wood. Then remove the old paint completely with a liquid paint remover or an electric paint softener (see page 41). Allow the surface to dry for a couple of days; then apply a primer that has a pigmented, waterproofing sealer. As a finish, use a water-base paint; it will allow any undetected moisture to work its way out without flaking the surface.

Priming the surface

Most paints are designed to be used over some type of priming

Safety Tips to Read Before Painting

A few basic cautions before you start to paint:

Be sure to check the labels on paint cans for warnings about possible hazards. Read them carefully —never ignore the instructions.

Like other toxic materials, paints and paint products should be kept out of the reach of children.

Always work with paint products in a well-ventilated area. Excessive inhalation of fumes from paints and solvents can cause dizziness, headaches, fatigue, and nausea. Also keep pets out of freshly painted rooms; paint fumes are especially harmful to pet birds.

Don't use or store paint products near a flame. Avoid smoking while painting or using solvents.

Clean up promptly after the job is finished and dispose of soiled rags.

Many paints and solvents are particularly harmful to skin and eyes. Be especially careful when handling or applying products that contain strong solvents—again, read the labels.

Inspect ladders for sturdiness. Check scaffolding planks for splits, cracks, or other weak points. Never lean away from a ladder—get off and move it if you can't easily reach a particular spot.

agent. The old finish, provided its condition is good, is usually all that's necessary. But in many cases an undercoat is required. Listed here are the situations requiring a primer, followed by the particular primer to use:

• Unpainted wood to be finished with enamel or oil-base paint—oil-base enamel undercoat.
• Unpainted wood to be finished with latex—oil-base undercoat.
• Unpainted plaster, plasterboard, drywall—latex paint or latex primer-sealer.
• Unpainted metal—rust inhibitive primer (each metal has its own particular primer).
• Rough, coarse, or porous masonry—block filler (a penetrating coating that fills holes).
• Dark-colored existing paint to be covered by light-colored finish coat—an extra coat of desired color or a primer.
• Light-colored existing paint to be covered by a dark finish coat—two coats of dark-colored paint.

Stirring the paint

The final step in preparation is stirring the paint. Most dealers will stir the paint for you at the time of purchase, especially if it has been custom colored. If the paint has been allowed to settle before application, though, it's best to stir it again just before you start painting.

If you plan to stir the paint at home, first check the label. A few newly developed paints should not be stirred. For paints that need it, begin by stirring up pigment that has settled at the bottom of the can. Continue stirring until there are no signs of color separation.

Never shake cans of varnish or polyurethane; if you do, you'll create bubbles that will last 4 or 5 days.

FOLLOW THE PROPER PAINTING SEQUENCE

That old joke about painting one's self into a corner is not based on fantasy: it can and does happen. You'll also want to avoid splattering paint onto newly painted surfaces or inadvertently touching a just-painted edge. To sidestep these plights, follow the painting sequence given below.

Painting the ceiling— section by section

Begin your project by painting the ceiling. Treat this as the big job it is —have a large roller and a 3 to 4-foot extension handle ready. If you find an extension handle awkward to work with, use a pair of ladders (or a sawhorse and ladder) and a scaffolding plank.

To avoid painting over any edge that may have dried (this causes lap marks), paint the entire ceiling (or ceiling section) without stopping. Make sure that the light is good enough so that you can see how completely you're covering. And wear a hat—you'll quickly discover why hats are so popular among professional painters. Wearing old clothes is also a good idea.

Paint in rectangles, approximately 2 by 3 feet. Starting in a corner, work across the ceiling in the direction of the shortest

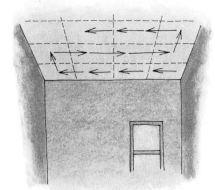

distance. Within each section, use a brush or corner roller to paint a narrow strip next to the wall line and around any fixtures. Then finish the section with a roller, overlapping any brush marks.

Painting walls— from one corner on

Next, paint the walls in 3-foot-square sections. Start from a corner at the ceiling and work down the wall. As with ceilings, paint the edge of each section with a brush or corner roller along the ceiling line, corners, and fixtures or edges of openings. Finish each section with a roller, overlapping any brush marks. At the bottom, use a brush and paint guide for the edge along the floor or baseboard, again overlapping edges with a roller. Return to the ceiling and work down again in successive 3-foot-square sections.

(Continued on page 48)

Painting with a Roller

Step 1. *Moisten the roller cover with the appropriate solvent (water for latex, thinner for oil-base), working it into the nap. Blot the cover with a cloth.*

Step 2. *Stir the paint thoroughly while it is still in the can (some paints don't require stirring; check the label first). Pour the paint into the roller tray until it is two-thirds full.*

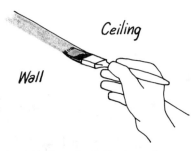

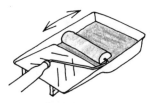

Step 3. *Mentally divide the wall or ceiling into approximately 3-foot-square areas. Where these areas meet a ceiling, wall, corner, or floor line, use a brush or corner roller to paint a narrow strip along the edge.*

Step 4. *Run your roller back and forth in the paint to soak it thoroughly.*

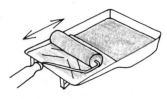

Step 5. *Pull the roller up the corrugated slope of the tray. The roller cover should be saturated but not drippy.*

Step 6. *Slowly roll paint onto the surface with light, even strokes in all directions; roll as close to edges and corners as possible in order to cover any textural differences between brush and roller marks. Caution: Reload the roller before it is completely empty.*

Step 7. *With an unloaded roller, roll over any overlap areas to even out the paint. Finish by rolling in one direction.*

Step 8. *Begin the next area away from the last finished area. When the new area is completed, roll slightly into the previously finished area, blending the overlap.*

Painting with a Pile Spreader

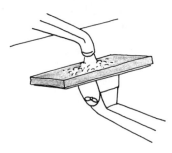

Step 1. *Lightly moisten the spreader pad with the appropriate solvent (water for latex, thinner for oil-base), working the solvent into the foam backing. Blot with cloth.*

Step 2. *Fill the roller tray or special pan-type paint tray (see directions for filling under "Painting with a roller," opposite). If you are using a roller tray, draw the paint up onto the corrugated slope of the tray with the edge of the spreader. Rock the spreader back and forth in the paint on the slope. If you are using a pan-type paint tray, dip only the absorbent pad of the spreader, flat-side down, about ¼ inch into the paint. Lift the spreader straight up and allow excess paint to drip off.*

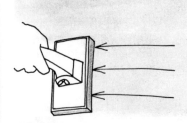

Step 3. *To apply paint, use long, smooth, pulling strokes in one direction. As you finish each stroke, tilt the handle edge of the spreader outward; this will produce a thin edge of paint for smooth blending with the next stroke.*

Painting with a Brush

Step 1. Roll the bristle ends between the palms of your hands to remove any loose bristles; shake the brush vigorously.

Step 2. Dampen the bristles thoroughly with the appropriate solvent (water for latex, thinner for oil-base). Wipe off excess moisture.

Step 3. Stir the paint until it is uniform in color and thickness; then pour it into a clean rimless pail until the pail is half full.

Step 4. Dip half the length of the bristles into the paint several times to thoroughly saturate the bristles.

Step 5. Dip the brush one-third to one-half the length of its bristles into the paint, gently stirring with the brush to spread the bristles slightly. (Do not stir on subsequent dippings.)

Step 6. Lift the brush straight up, allowing excess paint to drip back into the pail. Slap both sides of the brush gently against the inside of the pail two or three times. Note: Do not wipe the brush across the lip of the pail; this may cause the bristles to separate into clumps, and you'll have less paint on your brush.

Spread with smooth strokes

Blend with unloaded brush

New section

Step 7. Spread the paint with smooth, even strokes. On smooth surfaces, direct your final strokes one way. On rough surfaces, vary the direction to help fill crevices. On wood surfaces, final strokes should run parallel to the grain. Gradually release the pressure on the brush as you approach the end of each stroke. Paint out to an edge, not in from it.

Step 8. Blend brush marks by running an unloaded brush very lightly over the wet paint.

Step 9. Work in small areas; finish a 2 to 3-foot-wide strip before you start the next one. Begin a new strip a few inches away from the freshly painted area and blend into the previous strip.

...(Continued from page 45)

If you don't think you'll paint all the walls in a single day, finish the wall you're working on before you stop. This way you avoid having to paint over dry edges later (otherwise, lap marks will show up).

Painting the trim— the fine work

Painting trim demands patience. It is meticulous work—not to be hurried. Basic tools you'll need are a 1½-inch angular sash brush to paint narrow molding, a 2-inch trim brush to paint wider trim, a painting guide, and masking tape.

Begin with the trim closest to the ceiling and work down. Brush paint on smoothly and evenly, using a painting guide when you're next to another surface.

Save the baseboard for last. Paint the baseboard's top edge first and then the floor edge, using masking tape or a painting guide to cover

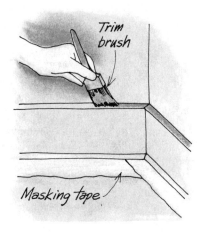

the edge of the floor. To paint the baseboard's vertical surface, use a wide brush.

Painting windows: tricks of the trade

The delicate business of painting windows has furrowed many painters' brows. In this section you'll find several tips for eliminating much of the difficulty.

A steady hand is the best tool for painting the wood parts of windows. Also important is the right brush—preferably an angled sash brush that reaches neatly into corners.

Resist the temptation to do a fast paint job, thinking you will scrape off excess paint later; with scraping you run the risk of permanently scratching the window glass. To avoid this possibility, it's best to cover the window edges with masking tape.

Double-hung window. To paint this kind of window, raise the inner window ¾ open and lower the outer window the same distance. Paint

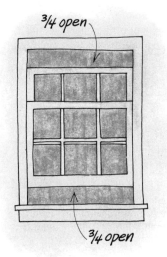

the outer window first, as follows. If your windows are paned, start by painting the horizontal muntins (pieces of molding that divide the window into sections), then the

vertical muntins, the exposed parts of the vertical sashes, and the bottom sash, in that order. Next, lower the inner window (don't close) and raise the outer window so that you can finish painting it. Finally, paint the inner window, starting with the muntins and finishing with the sashes.

The trim framing a double-hung window requires a few simple steps. Begin with the top frame, painting down the side frames. Paint the sill and its edge, sides, and bottom, finishing with the lower frame or sill apron. Allow the paint to dry completely. To prevent sticking, carefully move the top and bottom windows once or twice while the paint is drying.

Many windows are designed so that the entire sash can be easily removed from its casing for washing both the inside and the outside of the glass. You can use this feature to simplify painting—if weather conditions permit, remove the sashes and lay them on a table or other surface.

Painting windows flat is easier than painting them in their normal vertical position, particularly if a number of muntins are involved. Of course you have to be prepared to leave the windows out long enough to dry thoroughly.

Finally, wax the jamb (side lining)

—don't paint it because you're likely to have sticking problems later. With both windows lowered, wax the top half of the jamb and the visible sides of the lower half. Caution: If the window has metal jambs, the jamb should be left as is.

Casement window. Painting a casement window is much easier than painting a double-hung window. First, paint any vertical muntins and then any horizontal muntins. Continue by doing the top, bottom, and vertical sashes, in that order. Then paint the frame as you would the frame of a double-hung window.

Painting doors— on or off the hinges

A door can be painted on or off the jamb—the choice is up to you because the painting sequence is the same.

To remove a door, simply slip the hinge pins out—but never unscrew the hinges themselves. For painting, lean the door against a wall and place two small blocks of wood or rubber wedges under the bottom edge and a third wedge between the center of the top edge and the wall.

Or you can lay the door across sawhorses. Working on a horizontal surface allows you to flow on a good coat of paint without concern about the paint collecting in the lower corners of the panels and eventually dripping down. However, you do have to be careful not to apply too thick a coat or the paint may "puddle."

Standard procedure in painting doors is to move from top to bottom. For doors with inset panels, first paint the panel molding and the inside edges of the panel cavities. Next, paint the panels. Then

Panel edge

Panel

paint the horizontal and vertical strips around the panels. If the door opens into the room being

painted, paint the door's latch edge. If not, paint the hinge edge. Do not close the door (or rehang) until the paint is thoroughly dry.

The door frame is simple to paint. Begin with the top frame and work down on the side frames. If the door opens into the room, paint the jamb and the door side of the door stop. If the door opens away from the room, paint the jamb and the two surfaces of the door stop (see illustration above right). Keep the

Jamb

Stop

door ajar until the paint on the jamb is completely dry.

Painting cabinets— small-space maneuvering

The following steps for painting cabinets will help prevent accidental smears and spills. A brush with a shortened handle will also make it easier to paint small areas.

First, remove drawers and detachable shelves and place them on newspapers or drop cloths for painting separately. Next, start inside the cabinet. Paint the back wall, the shelf bottoms, the inside wall (working from the top down), and the shelf tops and edges, in that order.

Next, paint the outside surfaces of the cabinet, beginning at the top and working down.

Finally, paint the doors. Swing them open and paint the inside surfaces. Then push the doors nearly closed and paint the outside surfaces. *Caution:* Don't close the cabinet doors completely until the paint has dried.

TIP FROM THE PROS

The methods used to paint a supergraphic will vary with the form it takes, the colors and type of paint you plan to use, and other considerations. If you have in mind a supergraphic that you'd like to try, consult a paint dealer or graphic artist, or visit an art supply store.

CLEAN UP—THEN SIT BACK & ENJOY

Cleaning up after painting is a strangely satisfying finale; you're eager to put the room in order and sit back to enjoy the fruits of your labor. But in scrambling to bring your project to an end, don't overlook the need for cleaning and storing tools. Immediately after you finish using your tools, clean them. Don't wait—dry paint can make a later cleanup extremely difficult.

How to clean brushes

Clean brushes used in oil-base paints by following all the steps below. Omit steps 6 through 8 for natural-bristle brushes. Brushes used in latex paints are easier to clean, requiring that you follow only steps 6 through 11.

1) Remove excess paint from the brush with a scraper or by drawing the brush over a straightedge (not over the curved edge of a paint can).

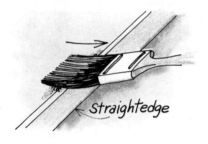
Straightedge

2) Pour a small amount of thinner into a container. Work the thinner through your brush, forcing it into the bristles—especially the heel.

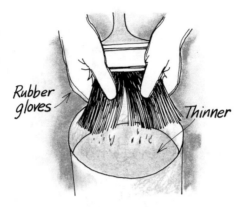
Rubber gloves — Thinner

3) When the thinner becomes saturated with paint, discard it and replace with new thinner. (Some people like to pour the used thinner into a can and save it. Paint will eventually sink to the bottom of the can, and the thinner can be reused. Label the can "First Wash.")

4) Repeat steps 2 and 3 until the thinner remains clear.

5) Shake the brush vigorously to remove excess thinner; another way is to lightly tap the handle against a hard edge.

6) Hold the brush under running water until the water runs clear.

7) Wash with soap and warm water, forcing water into the bristles and heel.

8) Rinse in warm running water.

9) Comb the bristles with a special comb made to keep bristles straight. Allow the brush to dry.

Bristle comb

10) Wrap the brush in its original covering or stiff paper.

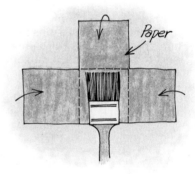
Paper

11) Store the brush by placing it on a flat surface or hanging it on a nail.

Short cuts to Make Painting Easier

● You'll find that rubbing your hands, arms, and face with hand lotion before painting makes paint spots easier to remove.

● To simplify cleanup of tools used in latex paint, occasionally rinse your brush or roller with water. This prevents paint buildup in the brush's bristles or the roller's nap.

● Here's an easy way to remove those bristles that come off as you are applying paint. Touch them with the tip of your wet brush—the bristles should stick to the brush. Use a cloth to wipe the stray bristles off the brush.

● A small magnet placed on the side of your metal paint bucket will keep your paint brush close at hand as you move around.

● A faster paint job is possible when two people work together. One person uses a roller to quickly roll on the paint while the other person follows, evening out the paint with a brush.

● No need to carry a heavy can of paint around when painting trim. Pour some paint onto the paint can lid—it's an easy-to-carry palette.

● Don't clean your brushes and rollers for short-term storage. Simply hang or place them in the appropriate thinner. Another trick is to wrap them in aluminum foil or plastic wrap.

How to clean rollers and spreaders

To clean these applicators, begin with the first two steps given below. If the applicator has been used to apply oil-base paint, continue with remaining steps, omitting steps 7 through 10. If latex was applied, skip steps 3 through 6 and start again at step 7.

1) Remove the excess paint from your roller or spreader with the edge of a putty knife. (You can

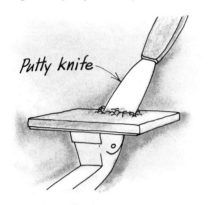

Putty knife

also squeeze out paint by pressing the roller against the lip of the tray.)

2) Remove the roller cover or spreader pad from its frame.

3) Pour thinner into a container. Wash the cover or pad, thoroughly forcing thinner into the nap.

4) Discard and replace the thinner when it becomes saturated with paint.

5) Repeat steps 3 and 4 until the thinner is clear.

6) Squeeze thinner from the cover or pad; then wash the roller or spreader frame in the thinner.

7) Hold the cover or pad under running water until the water runs clear.

8) Wash with soap and warm water, forcing water into the nap; then wash the frame.

9) Rinse the cover or pad and frame in warm running water.

10) Squeeze out excess water. Blot lightly with a clean, absorbent

cloth and set aside to dry completely.

11) Wrap cover or pad in a plastic bag or wrapping paper.

12) Store the roller cover on its end to prevent flattening the round surface.

Cleanup for other tools

First dispose of all soiled, inexpensive tools and equipment—painting guides, mixing paddles, plastic gloves, and drop cloths. Wipe off paint spatters from drop cloths you wish to keep, allow them to dry, and store them. With the appropriate solvent clean such preparation tools as scrapers, wire brushes, and putty knives; also clean miscellaneous painting tools—buckets and trays. Rinse well and allow to dry.

Paint storage

Most leftover paint can be stored in a tightly closed can for several months or more.

If less than a quarter of the paint in a can is remaining, transfer it to a container small enough to be almost filled (less air in the can means the paint has less chance of drying out); seal it tightly. Before covering a can of oil-base paint, pour a very thin layer of thinner on top of the paint.

Wipe off paint from the rim of the paint can to permit an airtight seal and to prevent paint from spattering when the lid is put on. Then firmly hammer on the lid.

Wipe off excess paint

Hammer on lid

It's best to store all solvents and other inflammable paints (check labels) in a metal cabinet.

Quick cleanup for yourself

Few painters can finish a paint job without having a few spatters land on themselves. But even the messiest painter need not despair—personal cleanup goes quickly.

Water-base paints come off easily with soap and warm water. Dried latex easily comes off your skin—but not your clothes. So wash your clothes before the paint has thoroughly dried.

Oil-base paint spots take a little more effort. For spots on arms and hands, lightly rub with thinner, working quickly. On face and neck, dab the spots off with a cloth dipped in thinner. Be extremely careful near the eyes. Then wash with soap and water, and to prevent your skin from drying after using thinner, be sure to apply a lotion to the cleaned areas.

Your glasses may also need cleaning. Latex spots can be washed off or—when the spots are dry—can be flicked off with a fingernail. Wipe off oil-base paint spots with thinner and rinse the glasses in warm water. Don't attempt to scrape the spots off; you may scratch the lenses, especially if they're plastic. Avoid using a solvent on plastic frames; it may remove or change the color.

Getting things together again

When the painted area has dried, you can return the room to its original condition.

Hopefully, if you've taken the time to carefully cover immovable objects and the carpet or floor, you won't find any paint spatters. Often, though, the most fastidious painter will find that a spot or two of paint has landed in the most unexpected place.

If you find this to be the case, carefully remove any smears, using thinner or water, depending on the paint. Remove any masking tape from windowpanes (use a paint scraper to remove any paint that may have seeped behind the tape) and plastic bags from doorknobs and other fixtures. Replace any doors, drawers, and shelves that have been removed. Also replace hardware and fixtures on doors, windows, cabinets, and walls.

EXTERIOR PAINTING—A SLIGHTLY DIFFERENT APPROACH

Painting a house exterior differs somewhat from painting an interior. You will need different paint, extra painting equipment, and some special techniques. You may also find exterior surfaces more difficult to prepare and paint because they often are weathered by sun, wind, rain, or snow.

When should you paint?

The right time to repaint a house is just before it needs painting—not after.

If you repaint too often, you'll end up with a too-thick coating that is brittle. The coating will be subject to cracking and flaking because it will not be able to adjust to structural movements of the house. On the other hand, if you allow the paint to deteriorate too badly, you'll find it harder to restore the surface to a good appearance.

Signs of a surface worn badly enough to warrant repainting include these: the wood grain becomes more pronounced; the primer shows through; the color fades.

Selecting the right paint

Listed below are some guidelines to help you select the best paint for the job. Before making a final decision, though, consult your paint dealer. Also, check the label on the paint can for possible warnings about painting in low or extremely high temperature and humidity levels—this advice can make or break a paint job.

Exterior oil-base paints

Oil-base paints are the preferred finishes for exterior surfaces where durability and gloss are required.
• Exterior oil-base enamels can be used on all properly primed wood and metal surfaces. They are especially recommended for wood siding, sash, trim, shutters, and doors. Metal surfaces include gutters, rails, and steel sash.
• Exterior flat finish is recommended primarily for rough siding,

board and batten, and cedar shingles and shakes. It can also be used on other properly primed surfaces and may be thinned enough for use as a heavy-bodied stain (however, a prepared stain will do a better job).
• Porch-and-deck paints are available for use on both concrete and wood surfaces. If the concrete surface is glossy, roughen it with muriatic acid before applying the paint; this will help the new paint adhere. Apply a primer to wood surfaces before painting with porch-and-deck paints.

Exterior latex paints

These paints have the same qualities as interior latex paints (see page 36). Latex is recommended for all exterior wood, masonry, stucco, and concrete surfaces. It is also suitable for galvanized metal and cement-asbestos boards.

Two special outdoor latex paints are available for certain situations —exterior latex trim enamel is used on exterior trim, doors, woodwork, and other areas of frequent contact; latex masonry paint is used to cover brick, stucco, concrete, and cinder block.

Spar varnishes

This is a large group of varnishes that are tougher than interior varnishes; they are recommended for such exterior surfaces as doors, sash, trim, and siding.

Penetrating wood stains

Highlighting the grain and texture of wood, these semi transparent stains are available in many hues. The most popular tones are cedar, light redwood, and dark redwood. These stains are available in both oil-base and water-base types.

Solid color stains

These products are thick enough to produce a near-opaque finish. They are available in either solvent-thinned or water-thinned types and in a wide range of colors.

Cement powder paint

This is a popular, low-cost finish for unpainted masonry and other unpainted rough surfaces, including brick, block, stucco, and concrete. It is a powder composed of white Portland cement, pigments, and a small amount of water repellent. Before application you add water to get the right consistency.

Tools and supplies

In addition to the brushes and rollers recommended for interior painting, you may need larger applicators for exterior surfaces. Block brushes—ranging from 4 to 6 inches wide—will help you to quickly cover large, flat surfaces. A big, thick-napped roller is another time-saving tool. And larger applicator pads are available for attachment to standard-size pile-spreader frames.

Also for these large areas, consider using a compressed-air spray painting system. Though it has limited use indoors because of overspray and fumes, outdoors it is a fast technique for painting your house. Check with your dealer for prices of rentals and sales. You may also wish to ask him about the "airless" spray unit. It is more expensive ($30 to $40 a day rental), but it produces a direct spray of pure paint without any overspray.

An extension ladder is a must for exterior painting, particularly for two-story homes. Remember, though, that the stability of this ladder is determined by the angle it makes with the wall. In placing an extension ladder, be sure that the horizontal distance from the wall to the foot of the ladder equals one-quarter of the working length of the ladder.

1/4 length of ladder

If the paint is badly worn, make surface preparation easier by using large scrapers, wire brushes, and an electric sander. And for other surface repairs you may need window sash putty, stucco or masonry patching compound, and a little carpentry skill.

Preparing the surface

As with interior painting, the most important part of exterior painting is surface preparation. Here is a check list of things you may need to do:

1) Take down light fixtures, mailboxes, hardware, screens, shutters, and house numbers for separate painting.

2) Repair any structural damage (see the *Sunset* book *Basic Home Repairs*).

3) Repair peeling, flaking, and mildew and remedy their causes (see directions on pages 43-44).

4) Reset or replace popped-out nails.

5) Roughen high gloss areas so the finish coat will adhere better.

6) Cover bare wood surfaces with a primer.

7) Seal open joints around windows and trim with a caulking compound.

8) Hose off dirt and excessive chalking of old paint.

9) Replace any loose or missing window putty.

10) Pull plants away from walls with rope or heavy twine and cover them with drop cloths.

11) Place drop cloths where necessary to protect patios, porches, and other floor surfaces.

Where do you start painting?

Because the color of the paint can change dramatically when exposed to the elements for a time, it is important that you finish painting the exterior of your house in one season. A good way to make sure you do this is to paint the back of the house first. That way, you'll have a continuing impetus to go on to finish the front for appearance's sake.

It's best to begin at the top of the house and work down, applying paint to areas within comfortable reaching distance as you stand on the ladder. Start with gutters, top portions of downspouts, eaves, peaks, gables, or porch ceilings. (Use rust-resistant paint for the inside of gutters.)

Eave

Don't apply paint too thickly to surfaces that are protected from the elements. Little wear occurs in

these places, and an overly thick coating will quickly crack and peel.

Still working from the top down, paint the house walls as you would interior walls (see illustration on page 45). On horizontal wood siding, apply paint to the bottom edges of two or three boards and then smooth out the paint on the flat surfaces. Force

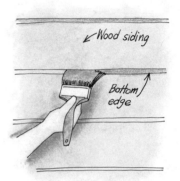

Wood siding

Bottom edge

Wood siding

Finish painting flat surface

paint into rough surfaces, such as shingles and shakes, to fill the crevices.

As you work down the ladder, leave a very lightly painted edge along areas you have finished. After you've moved the ladder and are painting another top-to-bottom strip, you'll paint over these light edges and not create a heavy overlap.

Paint the trim, windows, and doors, following the interior painting procedures (see pages 48-49).

Porches, patios, and steps are next (remember to leave one access to the house unpainted while the others are drying). Don't forget metal railings, ornamental iron, and other accessories.

Finally, paint the items you have removed from the house.

Multitude of choices

Dazzling selection of wallpapers makes final decision difficult. Weight of paper and ease of application are major factors to consider.

Outdoor feeling brought indoors

Scenic mural of woodsy setting adds color and depth to this living room wall. Sections of paper must be carefully hung to make invisible seams.

WALLPAPERING

"Busy as a one-armed paper hanger," the old saying went. But times do change, and today, certain developments in wallpapering simplify *anybody's* work in covering walls.

You'll find that neither professional skill nor experience is necessary to install wallpaper. More than half the people who buy wall coverings are homeowners and apartment dwellers who do their own papering. Many are starting their first decorating projects.

"Patience," counsel the professionals. It's true that watching your room change character as you cover the walls with a new pattern is the exciting part of the job. But don't skimp on adequate surface preparation—cleaning and patching. Unless you lay the groundwork for a smoothly papered wall, you may eventually end up with more wall drama than you planned for: blistering paper, mildew, and seam separation.

If you're about to embark on your first wallpapering job, you may feel hesitant about the scope of the project. The solution? Try covering a small, inconspicuous area with wallpaper—a wall niche, the end of a cabinet, a small alcove. You may be surprised at how well you do—and how much you enjoy it.

Leafing through these pages, you'll learn that wallpaper is far more sophisticated than it used to be. An early discovery may be that wallpaper isn't always paper.

A KALEIDOSCOPE OF WALLPAPERS

To say that wallpaper is not what it used to be is a striking understatement. Today's wallpaper includes almost any material that can be pasted up as a wall covering. And even the pasting process has changed; some wallpapers come prepasted. The old joke from the great 1930s Depression days—"Take down the wallpaper, we're moving"—has become a reality: you can now buy wallpaper that can be easily removed, then applied to another surface.

Oriental grasscloth, burlap, foil, vinyl, cork, felt, patterned sheets, carpeting—the list of wall covering materials is impressive. Even more varied is the array of patterns. You can cover your wall with scenic murals, blown-up painting reproductions, geometrics, and abstracts. Among all of the available wall finishings, wallpaper has become the most versatile.

Perhaps you will spend days thumbing through samples of wallpaper designs. But once you've decided on material and pattern, the actual hanging may take only a weekend.

Standard wallpaper is the old favorite

Standard wallpapers are normally printed either on a machine roller or by a handprinted silk-screen process. Both methods can create patterns with subtle shading and feeling of depth.

Standard papers can cost from less than $5 a roll to many times that amount if they are the work of a top designer.

Machine-printed papers are generally pretrimmed. Silk-screened papers may come pretrimmed but usually have selvage edges that need to be trimmed before the paper is hung. On silk-screened papers, pattern alignment is not machine precise.

Note that, when you select standard wallpaper, the cheapest paper is not always the best buy. Because it is generally pulpy and

Pattern *of this vinyl-coated wallpaper convincingly simulates decorative tile.*

porous, inexpensive wallpaper absorbs moisture too readily, causing the paper to tear easily during installation. (For installation tips, see pages 68-72.)

Foil wallpaper—for shine

Foil wallpaper is a very thin, flexible metallic sheet—either aluminum or simulated metal—laminated to a paper or fabric

Which to choose? *Wallpapers come in a parade of colors and patterns. The notepad in this customer's hand lists room dimensions, other facts for reference when shopping.*

Striking, bold pattern *of mylar-coated foil adds to the intensity of this wallpaper.*

Wallpapering Terms You Should Know

Air bubbles/Blistering. A bubble of trapped air or a paste lump under wall covering.

Bolt. Two or more rolls of wallpaper in a single package.

Booking. After pasting a strip, folding it inward by thirds so that the pasted cut ends meet and the edges exactly align.

Border. A narrow decorative strip of paper, usually placed at the joining of the wall and ceiling.

Companion fabric. A fabric that has been printed in the same pattern as that on a wall covering. Because of differences in materials, dyes, and printing processes, the color values in companion fabrics are rarely identical to those in wallpaper.

Companion papers. A set of two papers usually designed or colored to coordinate decoration in one room or adjoining rooms. One paper may consist of a large, bold pattern, the other a stripe or other semiplain effect, both with the same coloring.

Lining paper. An inexpensive blank paper stock recommended for use under foils and other fine quality coverings. Lining paper absorbs excess moisture.

Pattern repeat. The vertical distance between a point of a pattern and the next point where the pattern is identical.

Prepasted paper. A wall covering that has been covered at the factory with a water-soluble adhesive. Instead of pasting it before hanging, you simply soak it in water.

Pretrimmed. Rolls of wallpaper from which selvage has been trimmed at the factory.

Run number. Since separate printings of a pattern may vary in color and intensity, each printing is designated with a different run number shown on the bolt package. If you have to order additional wallpaper after your first purchase, always specify the desired run number as well as the pattern number.

Selvage. The edges of wallpaper or fabric covering that are trimmed off before paper is hung. Selvages carry no design but are intended to protect the paper and carry instructions for its use.

Size (also sizing). A commercially available liquid coating that helps seal prepared surfaces, provides a cohesive bond between paste and wall, and allows the installer to move the wall covering into position more easily.

Strip. A length of wallpaper cut to fit the height of a wall. In scenics, a single section of the design.

Strippable paper. A type of wallpaper that can be removed without tearing and without the use of water or steam.

Vinyl-to-vinyl adhesive. A special adhesive used for joining one vinyl surface to another.

Washable. A term to indicate that a wall covering can be cleaned with a mild soap and water without being damaged by it. The term does not assure that soil, grease, or stains are removable. Washability varies with different wallpapers.

---

back. Some foils are coated with mylar to give them a highly reflective mirror finish.

Foils are printed in many colors. Some are mottled to resemble marble or tortoise shell, a gilt-etched mirror, or other light-reflecting surfaces. Others have bold, new patterns.

The price of foils ranges from moderate (you won't find a roll that costs under $10) to expensive.

(For installation pointers, see pages 72 - 73.)

Vinyl wallpaper is durable

Vinyl wallpaper is either a flexible film or a liquid bonded by heat to a paper or fabric backing material.

Vinyl wall coverings range in price from under $10 a roll to moderately expensive.

(Continued on next page)

Vinyl paper has durable and scrubbable finish—a prime factor in choosing wallpaper for a child's room.

Eye-catching poster pattern invites visitors to read fine print on vinyl wallpaper. Interior design: Wallpapers to Go.

. . . Continued from page 57

The most durable of all wall coverings, vinyl wallpaper is far more scrubbable and resistant to damage than the rest. Ask your dealer about the difference between vinyl wallpapers and papers that are only vinyl-coated. The latter are not particularly wear-resistant, grease-resistant, or washable. (For installation pointers, see page 73.)

Flocked wallpaper—the elegant one

This two-dimensional paper is produced by a machine that shakes finely chopped nylon or rayon fibers over paper on which a pattern has just been printed with

Raised pattern of flocked wallpaper offers interesting shading to the eye and texture to the touch.

slow-drying paint. The texture of the finished paper resembles that of damask or cut velvet.

Flocks start at less than $10 a roll and can cost up to three times that much. The range of available patterns and colors is wide. (For installation pointers, see page 72.)

Fabric coverings for one-of-a-kind walls

As a unique way to add interest to walls, fabrics have recently become popular—though often expensive—wall coverings.

Any fabric of your choice can be laminated to paper for hanging; inquire about this service in an interior design shop. If you're interested in matching your beddings, drapes, or upholstery to your wallpaper, ask your dealer about companion fabrics.

Coordinated wallpaper and drapes add a feeling of unity to room decor and a touch of elegance to traditional look. Interior design: Albert Van Luit & Co.

Note that, whenever you use a patterned fabric as a wall covering, it is almost impossible to exactly match the pattern as you hang each strip of material. (For installation pointers, see page 73.)

Patterned sheets as wall coverings

A great advantage of patterned sheets as a wall covering is that it is considerably less costly to cover a wall with sheets than with many other fabrics. Another point in favor of patterned sheets is their high style; you can get a real decorating boost by using sheets that have been designed by leading artists. (For ideas on the kinds of patterned sheets available, look first at the colorful sheeting advertisements in home magazines and department store brochures.) See the back cover of this book for an illustration of sheets used as a wall covering.

More fabric wall coverings and ideas

Shopping in yardage stores can help spark your imagination. Perhaps silk, muslin, linen, or synthetics will suit your wall-covering fancy.

You can line a sewing room wall with pockets of corduroy for storing small materials or decorate it with muslin pattern pieces in different colors. Think how a playroom would come alive if its walls were given a patchwork covering.

Oriental weaves and natural textures

Walls are often enriched by coverings of exotic weaves and natural textures. (For installation pointers, see page 74.)

Oriental weaves: grasscloth, burlap, and hemp

The three most popular oriental weaves—grasscloth, burlap, and hemp—are widely used in home decorating. All are available laminated on paper backing.

A roll of woven material may cost under $20 or it can cost hundreds of dollars, depending on the type of weave and the site from which it was imported.

Though many oriental weaves have no particular pattern, some are manufactured with such patterns as basketweave and herringbone. Some even have a decorative pattern printed on the face of the texture. The color uniformity of all oriental weaves varies slightly.

Grasscloth lets you go native. Since grasscloth has no pattern, you'll have no matching problem

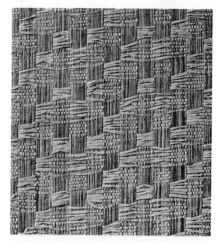

Roughly woven grasscloth, laminated to paper backing, offers hint of faraway places.

when installing it. As with most weaves, it is natural for the seams of this material to show.

Real grasscloth is made from arrowroot bark imported from Japan. Because of the shortage of this bark, though, synthetic materials are now often substituted for real grasscloth.

Burlap has become respectable. It has been a long upward climb for burlap since the days when it served chiefly as sacking for rice. Now you can buy natural or colored burlap in bolts and cut it in strips to cover your wall. Burlap on which patterns have been silk-screened is also available in many colors.

Heavily textured *cork veneer wallpaper has warm, earthy quality. Most types are relatively expensive, making installation by a professional advisable.*

Silhouette *of branches and flowers lends touch of tranquility to this burlap wallcovering.*

Since the color uniformity of burlap doesn't vary as much as that of grasscloth or hemp, seams are less noticeable. Because of its neutral color, natural burlap blends well with other colors.

Burlap is an ideal surface on which to hang pictures or notes because it doesn't show tack marks.

Hemp: grasscloth's cousin. Though hemp resembles grasscloth, it has a much finer weave. Still, it contains all the natural irregularities and color variations of grasscloth, and the seams will be prominent.

Natural textures: cork and wood veneers

You can get exciting results from "papering" your walls with cork or a wood veneer. Because both materials are tricky to install, it's best to let a professional do the job.

Cork is a winner. The natural shading properties of cork add to the beauty of this material. Paper-backed cork wall covering comes in a variety of thicknesses and weights. It is also available in many patterns—among them diamond, parquet, and stripe.

Wood veneers can be expensive. If you're fond of natural wood grain, would you like an alternative to installing board or sheet paneling? To achieve a similar look, consider a paper-backed or cloth-backed wood-veneer wall covering. These wood-veneer papers, available in a variety of woods, effectively display the natural wood grain. But they can be costly.

Burlap *covers the walls of boy's bedroom. This fabric is a good choice because of durability, color range, low cost, and ease of application.*

Scenic murals and special mountings

Scenic murals are handscreened, machine-printed, or lithographed pictorial designs pieced together in several strips of wallpaper. Special mountings can take the form of a blown-up Picasso painting or even a family photograph enlarged many times to fit the wall dimensions.

There's an enormous range in price for scenic murals and special mountings. Some ready-made photo murals cost under $50 in either color or black and white. But top designer scenic murals and most special mountings can cost hundreds of dollars.

Since murals are printed on varying kinds of wall covering materials, installation methods will vary (see "How to hang the first strip," page 68, and "Different wall coverings—different installations," page 72).

Before hanging a special mounting, be sure to check with your wallpaper dealer about the best way to hang the print. Above all, be certain that the print will fit the area you want to cover.

Sometimes the expense of special mountings and scenic murals is such that you may want to have them installed by a professional.

Scenic murals expand your horizons

Murals often have as their subject matter a natural setting—farm lands, a seascape, or a view from a mountain top. They can also portray a historical setting—ancient Rome, for example. Sometimes a mural is a symbolic picture, such as one showing the history of the United States from the time of Columbus through the era of the astronauts.

Murals in both black and white and color are sold in some wallpaper stores, or you can find them in the shops of interior designers.

Special mountings— the show stoppers

These are the custom-designed show stoppers of the wall covering industry. Photographs of real scenes or paintings enlarged to wall size, they can be among the most expensive of wall coverings. Color enlargements cost three times as much as black and white.

Special mountings can be silk-screened on a variety of materials —paper, vinyl, linen, mylar, jute, burlap, grasscloth, cork, and others.

You can have a special mounting made by professionals at a studio

Life-size memories *transform this door; blowup was made from 35mm negative.*

specializing in general graphics (listed under "Photo Copying" in the Yellow Pages). They will make giant photos from 4 by 5 negatives, positive prints, 35mm slides, material from books or magazines, or original graphic material.

In processing color mountings, the dealer must intensify color in the reproduction because the increase in photo size reduces the density of the negative's color. There's an added cost for this.

Carpeting

Both lightweight standard and indoor-outdoor carpeting are occasionally used as wall coverings. When installed on a wall, carpeting requires little maintenance, shows no scrapes or scratches, and reduces noise considerably.

Carpets come in a wide choice of patterns and textures and span a broad price range. Dealers will recommend specific techniques for attaching carpeting to walls.

Black and white mural *showing classical European scene covers folding screen that can be placed to accent a room or conceal an area. Interior design: Wallpapers Inc.*

Helpful Wallpapering Tools

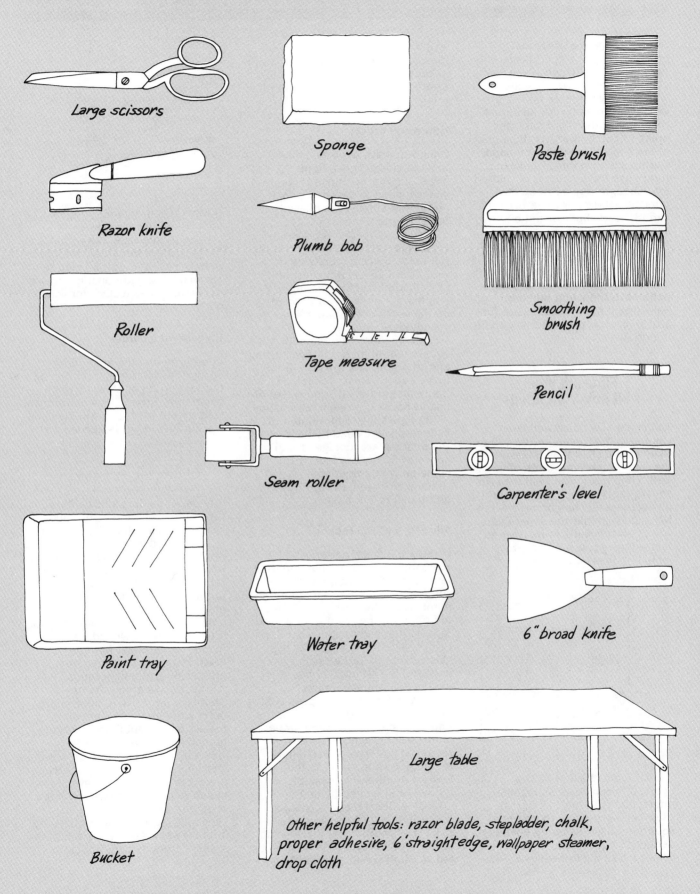

Large scissors

Sponge

Paste brush

Razor knife

Plumb bob

Smoothing brush

Roller

Tape measure

Pencil

Seam roller

Carpenter's level

Paint tray

Water tray

6" broad knife

Bucket

Large table

Other helpful tools: razor blade, stepladder, chalk, proper adhesive, 6' straight edge, wallpaper steamer, drop cloth

It pays to make a generous estimate of your paper needs when purchasing wallpaper. If you run short of paper during installation, you may have trouble finding an exact color match with additional rolls. And if there are damaged areas to patch later, you'll be glad to have matching paper on hand. During each printing, manufacturers use fresh batches of colored ink. Though they try to exactly duplicate the color of earlier runs, variations in shade or tint often occur.

Each newly mixed batch of color is identified by a run number that is printed on the package of each wallpaper bolt. Be sure that all your bolts have the same number. Selecting the proper adhesive for attaching your wallpaper is equally important.

Figuring your wall covering needs

To decide how much wallpaper you need, first measure the wall or room with a steel tape. Measure the total height and width of each wall. Then figure the total area (in square feet) of each wall by multiplying the wall's height by its width. Now add together the square footage of all the walls to be covered; this will give you the total area, including wall openings.

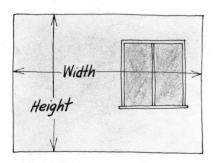

Most rooms have windows, doors, a fireplace, or some other interruptions in the wall space. After you figure up a room's total square footage including openings, deduct 15 square feet for every average-size door or window. For larger or unusually shaped openings, measure the height and width of each opening and deduct the exact square footage from your total.

How many rolls?

Once you learn the total square footage of wall space to be covered (with openings deducted), you will need to determine the number of single rolls of wallpaper needed.

Though wallpaper is priced by the single roll, it is sold in multiple-roll bolts. Since papers vary in width from 18 to 54 inches, bolts of wallpaper contain varying lengths of paper—it all depends on the width of the paper you choose.

Each single roll contains 36 square feet of material. The cutting and trimming you will do will deduct about 6 square feet, so figure on getting 30 square feet of usable paper from each roll you buy.

You figure the total number of single rolls you need by dividing the total square footage of wall space by 30 square feet. If you come up with a fractional remainder of square feet, buy an additional roll of paper.

Allow for pattern repeat

If you are using a patterned wallpaper, one additional important bit of calculation remains if you are to accurately estimate the number of rolls you need. That is to figure out the number of pattern repeats that will fit your actual wall height. Note that a drop match (see "How to cut patterned paper," page 66) is half the number of inches of a pattern repeat.

To allow for pattern repeat, first divide the height (in inches) of the wall to be covered by the number of inches between the pattern repeat; if you have a fractional remainder, round it off to the next highest number. For example, a 96-inch wall height divided by an 18-inch pattern repeat gives you 5.33 repeats; this is rounded off to 6. Then multiplying the 18-inch pattern repeat by 6 repeats will tell you that 6 repeats will fit on a

Number of inches between

9-foot (108-inch) wall—not on your 8-foot (96-inch) wall.

If, as in this case, the actual wall height differs from the height your pattern repeat requires, plan to purchase the additional number of necessary rolls to allow for your pattern repeats.

If you want a border

In determining the amount of border needed for a room, divide the total width of all walls to be papered by three. Since borders are sold by the yard, this will give you the number of yards needed.

Choosing an adhesive

Wallpaper dealers stock adhesives for every possible type of wall covering installation. Before you select an adhesive, read the wallpaper manufacturer's instructions to learn which adhesive he recommends, or ask your dealer for one that is suitable for your material.

Adhesives come in both dry and premixed forms. Dry adhesive is made from a wheat formula; premixed is made from a non-organic or synthetic formula.

You can use either dry or premixed adhesive to apply such porous materials as standard papers and oriental weaves. But to install nonporous papers—vinyls, foils, mylars, and other specially treated materials—use premixed adhesive; its low moisture content makes it mildew resistant. This adhesive is an especially good choice for hanging oriental weaves—it won't separate a weave from its paper or cloth backing.

PREPARING THE SURFACE

Before wallpapering, you will want to make sure that a wall is completely clean and totally free from damage.

Among the preparatory steps you may have to take are removing wall lighting fixtures and the plates from electrical switches and outlets, repairing all cracks and holes, stripping the old wall covering (if there is one), cleaning and rinsing the wall thoroughly, and applying a primer-sealer.

How you clean and prepare your wall for papering depends on the type of wall, its condition, and the kind of paper you are installing. Here is how you approach preparing different kinds of walls:

Preparing an already papered wall

If your existing wallpaper is in good condition, only one layer, and not flocked, you can probably paper over it successfully after a few preparatory steps—with this exception: if you plan to hang a nonporous paper, most wallpaper manufacturers recommend that you completely remove old wallpaper.

If you leave old paper on the wall. Once you've established that the paper already on the wall is basically in good condition, check it for air bubbles (puncture them) or loose corners or seams and glue them down with the same adhesive you will use to install the new paper.

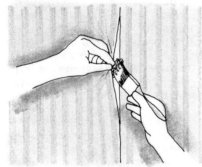

Carefully check old seams; if necessary, sand and fill with spackling compound (see page 42). Fill all cracks and holes with spackle or patching plaster and

sand when dry. Apply one coat of flat oil-base enamel undercoat to the wall; allow this to dry for 24 hours. Check the directions that come with the wallpaper to find out if you need to size the wall (see page 57) before hanging the paper.

If the existing paper is a foil or a specially treated, nonstrippable material or if your old wall covering is a cloth-backed vinyl that has been hung over gypsum wallboard without a sealer, then you must apply a special vinyl-to-vinyl primer to the wall before papering.

If you remove old paper. Wallpaper in poor condition, multiple layers of wallpaper, and flocked wallpaper must be removed before you hang a new paper. If your existing wallpaper is a modern, strippable one, it will come off easily when you pull up at a corner or seam.

Beginning at one corner, carefully pull strip from wall

TIP FROM THE PROS

Repairing a damaged area of wallpaper is easy. Set a piece of new wall covering over the damaged area, carefully matching the pattern. Cut an irregularly shaped patch (it will be less noticeable than a square shape) from the new piece, simultaneously cutting through the wallpaper on the wall. Remove the damaged piece, following directions that begin on this page; place the pasted patch in place.

Before removing nonstrippable existing paper, break the surface of the paper by sanding it with very coarse sandpaper or scoring the wall with a saw (scrape the saw's entire cutting blade against the paper in many places—and in any direction).

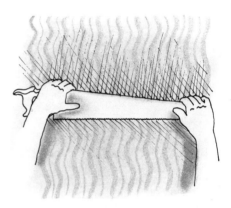

To remove the wallpaper, you can use a steamer or a garden sprayer. With either tool you can add a liquid (ask your dealer) to hasten the paste-dissolving process.
● A wallpaper steamer converts water to steam that runs through a hose to a pan with a trigger. You move the pan slowly along the wall, allowing the steam to penetrate the paper. You can rent —or perhaps borrow—one from your dealer.

Steamer

(Continued on next page)

. . . Continued from page 63

• A hand or tank garden sprayer can be used to spray a fine mist of extremely hot water onto the paper; allow it to penetrate.

Both of the above methods will soften the old paste in a matter of minutes. When this happens, use a broad knife to remove the paper.

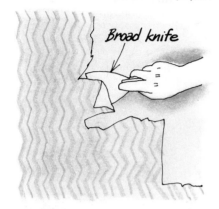

Broad knife

Begin at the top of the wall and work downward. If the paper does not pull away easily, dampen it again. Do not force it with the knife; work carefully to avoid nicking or chipping the wall's surface.

In cases where the wall has been covered with several layers of paper, you will find it easier to remove one layer at a time. If a nonporous sealer was used on any one of these layers, first sand it or score it in many places with a saw blade before using a steamer or garden sprayer. After applying water or steam, allow time for the paper to loosen and then peel it off. (Since nonporous sealers are not water soluble, you must get the water behind the paper before it can effectively loosen the paste.)

If you find that the original layer of paper was applied directly to the wall and cannot be removed without damaging the wall, stop at that layer. Allow the wall to dry thoroughly (for at least 12 hours) and apply one coat of flat, oil-base enamel undercoat. Spackle any nicks you may have made in removing previous layers of paper; then sand smooth and seal again. Finally, size, if necessary (see page 57), and hang the paper.

Wallpaper pasted directly to gypsum wallboard without an undercoat of a nonporous sealer will be almost impossible to remove without damaging the wallboard. Sealing the wall with an undercoat of flat, oil-base enamel is the answer to this problem.

Preparing a newly plastered wall

A freshly plastered wall must be thoroughly dry (the type of plaster used will dictate the drying time—ask your builder) before it is covered. When the wall is completely cured, seal it with one coat of two-pound cut shellac or flat, oil-base primer-sealer; allow to dry. Size, if necessary (see page 57), and hang the paper.

Preparing a new dry wall

Before papering over a new dry wall (gypsum wallboard), tape and spackle all joints between panels with joint cement. When dry, sand

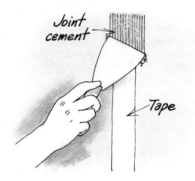

Joint cement

Tape

smooth and apply one coat of flat, oil-base primer-sealer. When the primer is dry, size the wall, if necessary (see page 57).

Preparing a painted wall

Wallpaper is often applied to plaster or wallboard surfaces that have been previously painted. If your old painted wall is not in need of repair, simply clean off all dirt, grease, and oil, and let it dry. (To repair holes and other surface damage, see details beginning on page 42.) If the existing paint is a flat, oil-base one, size, if necessary (see page 57), and hang the paper. But if it is latex paint, apply a coat of oil-base primer-sealer. If you don't know what type of paint was applied, use a flat, oil-base sealer.

Preparing a wood wall

To be successfully papered over, a wood wall must be flat and smooth.

For directions on preparing a rough or textured wall, see below. Tape and fill all joints and cracks with joint cement. If the wood has a wax finish on it, remove all wax. Then sand the surface and apply a flat, oil-base enamel undercoat.

Preparing a textured wall

Many gypsum wallboard and plaster walls are textured; some wood walls have rough finishes. These should be smoothed before you paper them. The most efficient way to do this is to cover the wall with a coat of gypsum joint compound and then sand after the compound dries. Finally, apply a coat of flat, oil-base primer-sealer; after it has thoroughly dried (about 24 hours), the wall will be ready for wallpaper.

Note that hanging lining paper (see page 57) over a textured wall will not make the surface smooth.

Preparing a concrete or cement-product wall

Concrete walls are found in some modern condominiums and high-rise buildings. Before any wall covering can be applied to these walls, you must remove all dirt

TIP FROM THE PROS

If you're using lightweight or porous paper, profit from these "don'ts":

1) Don't paper over dark painted walls; they could show through. Lighten them with a flat, oil-base enamel undercoat before hanging the paper.

2) Don't paper over dark paper or patterns. First lighten the background with paint or lining paper.

3) Don't paper over wallpaper if the ink comes off; it could bleed through the new paper. To test, moisten a small piece of the paper with a sponge. If the ink comes off, seal the old paper first with a pigmented shellac.

and grease (see page 42 for a recommended cleaner). When walls are clean and thoroughly dry, apply one coat of a flat, oil-base pigmented sealer. When this has dried, follow with one coat of oil-base enamel undercoat or acrylic primer.

Sometimes a cement wall will be so roughly textured that furring (see page 24) and adding wallboard or plastering over it is the only way to make it flat enough for application.

If you decide to plaster rather than to fur, follow the steps for preparing newly plastered walls (see opposite page) before hanging the wall covering.

Below-grade concrete walls, such as those found in basements and in lower levels of many split level homes, should be furred and covered with wallboard. This will provide a sound foundation for wall coverings and will help to insulate the room.

Preparing a mildewed wall

Mildew is primarily caused by a fungus living on damp, organic material. These spores cause staining of walls and other surfaces. Before you hang a wall covering, you must remove all existing fungal spores (and any wallpaper, see page 63). The most effective method is to scrub all infected areas with the following solution:

⅔ cup trisodium phosphate
⅓ cup strong detergent
1 quart bleach
3 quarts warm water

Follow this application by rinsing with clean water to remove all residue of the washing solution. After walls are thoroughly dry (about 24 hours), apply one coat of flat, oil-base enamel undercoat into which you have mixed a commercially available fungicide additive. When walls have dried, they will be ready for papering.

HANGING THE PAPER

The following pages take you through the basic steps for hanging standard wallpaper. However, for exceptions to the rules, see "Different wall coverings—different installations" beginning on page 72. Also, you will find wallpaper dealers to be a friendly group, ready to offer advice. Some dealers even conduct lectures or show films on techniques of hanging paper.

Create a working space

When you've donned your working clothes, provide yourself with a spacious work area. Do this by moving as much furniture out of the way as you can and covering the rest.

You will need a table large enough to hold your wallpaper strips. Put your stepladder into place and clear a path between the pasting table and the foot of the ladder. Put drop cloths or papers down to protect the carpet or floor from dripping paste. Next, make sure you have all the necessary tools (see page 61).

Where to begin

You will need to give some thought to where on a wall will be the best place to hang your first strip. Because the last strip you hang probably won't match the first, plan to finish hanging the paper in the least conspicuous place. Usually—if your room has no special openings such as a fireplace or picture window—the best place to begin is at a corner, a door casing, or a window casing on the wall that is least noticeable, moving around the room to the point where you began.

Here, though, are some suggestions on where to start if you find you have some common (and often puzzling) wall situations:

Wall with two windows. When papering a wall with two windows, locate the first strip between the two windows, not at the wall's corner. You can do this in either of two ways: 1) Position the edge of the strip between the windows at one casing; or 2) Position the center line of the strip between the two windows.

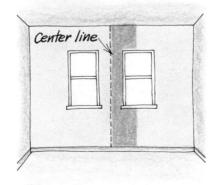

Wall with a fireplace or picture window. On a wall with a fireplace or picture window, hang the first strip of wallpaper above the fireplace or window. Do this in either of two ways: 1) Position the edge of

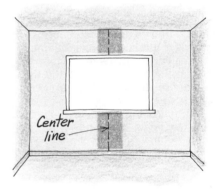

the strip at the center of the fireplace or picture window, or 2) Position the strip's center line at the center of the fireplace or window.

Establishing plumb

Most house walls are not straight and plumb (perfectly vertical). So, when applying wallpaper, instead of aligning the paper with a corner that is perhaps imperfectly vertical, you'll want to establish a plumb line.

First, locate where to put the line: figure your wallpaper's width less ½ inch, measure this distance from a corner, window, door, or some other starting point, and mark the wall there.

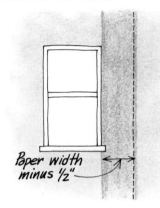

Paper width minus ½"

Now you're ready to establish plumb. You can do it in either of the two following ways:

1) If you have a carpenter's level, hold it flat against the wall, vertically aligning one edge with the mark. Adjust the level until the bubble that designates plumb is centered. Draw a line along the level's edge, straight down from your mark. Continue this process, connecting lines until you have a floor-to-ceiling plumb line.

2) You can also establish plumb using a plumb bob or a weight at the end of a string on which you've rubbed soft chalk. Locate where to put the line as described above, making a mark at the ceiling line. Place a tack in the wall at the mark and tie the string's end to the tack so that the plumb bob's point (or the weight's point) dangles a fraction of an inch above the floor. Once it stops swinging back and forth, press the lower end of the string against the wall and snap the line.

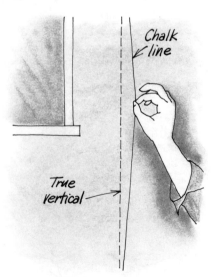

Chalk line

True vertical

If you plan to paper the ceiling, you will need to establish a guideline. To do this, measure in from the corner of the room about ½ inch less than the width of the paper to be hung. Mark the ceiling at that point. Now move to the opposite side of the room and measure in the same distance from the opposite corner; mark the ceiling at this point also. Snap a chalk line between the two marks.

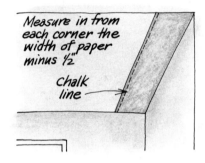

Measure in from each corner the width of paper minus ½"

Chalk line

Inspecting, matching patterns, cutting, pasting

Before you get into the irrevocable step of cutting strips of wallpaper, take these preliminary steps:

Make an inspection and take inventory

Most wall coverings come with specific directions prepared by the manufacturer. Be sure to read the directions all the way through before you open the first package of wall covering.

Before starting to measure and cut the paper, you should examine each bolt, making sure the run numbers (see page 62) match and checking for flaws in printing and variations in shading of the paper.

The next step is to take the vertical curl out of the paper. Do this by pulling out 3 to 4 feet of paper at a time and drawing this length firmly over a table edge,

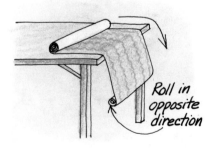

Roll in opposite direction

face side up. Then reroll the paper so that it curls in the opposite way from the way it was packaged.

If you find any defective material, immediately take it back to the store for replacement. Do this for two reasons: 1) No wall covering manufacturer or retailer will accept responsibility for defects after the product is on the wall; 2) If you delay, you may not find your pattern, texture, and color in the same run number.

How to cut patterned paper

There are basically two kinds of patterns: 1) Straight match and 2) Drop match. In straight match patterns, the same part of the

Straight match

pattern should be the same distance from the ceiling on each strip. Drop match patterns, on the other hand, alternate. Every other strip has a pattern the same distance from the ceiling.

Drop match

Before you cut, study the pattern to determine how you want it to appear on the wall. After you decide which match pattern you will use, you're ready to measure the strips and cut them from the roll. You will need a fairly large table to match the strips side by side.

Because ceiling heights can vary, it's a good idea to measure the wall height before cutting each strip of paper. Transfer this measurement to the paper, leaving 2 inches extra at the top and bottom.

Pasting: do-it-yourself . . . or is it already done?

Some wall coverings come with paper or cloth backing that needs to be spread with a paste; other coverings are prepasted and need only soaking in water before being hung.

If you use unpasted wall coverings. You can buy paste in wallpaper stores, hardware stores, or sometimes in lumberyards. Make certain that you choose the proper adhesive for your type of wall covering (see "Choosing an adhesive," page 62). Mix it in a bucket according to manufacturer's directions. Since directions vary from product to product, be sure to read them all the way through.

Paste should be mixed until it is even and not too thick. Get rid of all lumps—mix until the texture is smooth throughout. (You may have to squish a lump or two between thumb and forefinger.)

You apply paste to a strip of wall covering with a wide, soft paint roller or pasting brush just before hanging. (If your work is interrupted by an emergency, you don't want to have several already-pasted strips waiting to be hung.)

The goal in pasting is to cover the back of the wall covering completely, smoothly, and evenly without smearing any paste on the pattern side.

Follow these steps:
1) Place the strips for one wall in the center of your worktable, pattern side down. Align the first

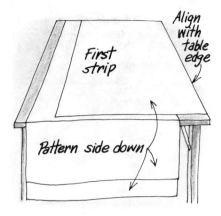

First strip

Align with table edge

Pattern side down

strip to be hung with the edge of the table.
2) With your brush or roller, apply paste evenly to the back of

Apply paste evenly

the first strip. (Excess paste that laps over the edges will be caught by the back of the next strip.) Work from the center toward the edge with an outward stroke. Be sure that enough paste is applied to the edges.
3) Fold the bottom third or more over the middle of the panel, pasted sides together, taking care not to crease the paper sharply at the fold. Be sure that edges are aligned.

Don't crease folds

Align edges

4) Fold the remaining portion of the pasted strip to meet the other cut end. (These last two steps are called "booking.")
5) If necessary, trim off the selvage. Place the pasted and booked strip (its edges aligned precisely) on the table. On one side, align a straightedge with the trim marks. Use a razor knife to cut through

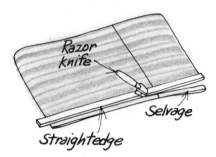

Razor knife

Selvage

Straightedge

both layers. Turn the strip around and follow the same procedure for the opposite side.

You are now ready to hang the strip. For specific directions, see the next page.

If you use prepasted wall coverings. Soak prepasted wall coverings in water for varying amounts of time, depending on the manufacturer's recommendations. Here's how to do it:
1) Place a water tray (a commercially available long and narrow tray, often of plastic) directly beneath the wall area that the first strip will cover. Fill the tray half full with lukewarm water.
2) Starting at the bottom of your cut wallpaper strip, roll it up with the pattern side in.
3) Submerge this roll in the water tray. Leave it submerged for 30 seconds or longer—depending on specifications.
4) Grasp the top of the soaked strip and pull it up toward the ceiling; then follow directions given on the next page for hanging the paper.

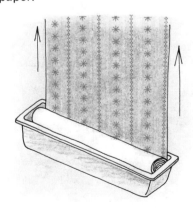

How to Hang the First Strip

Step 1. *Position the ladder next to the plumb line (see page 65).*

Step 2. *Open the top fold of the strip, raising it so that it overlaps the ceiling line 2 inches.*

Step 3. *Carefully align the strip's edge with the plumb line.*

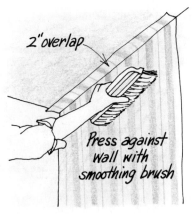

Step 4. *Press the strip against the wall, using a smoothing brush.*

Step 5. *Brush with a down-and-out stroke, moving from the center of the panel. Smooth out wrinkles and air bubbles.*

Step 6. *Release the lower half of the strip and smooth it into place.*

Step 7. *Use a seam roller to carefully roll the edges flat if necessary.*

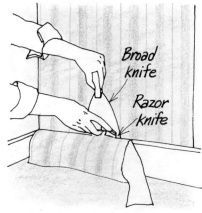

Step 8. *Trim the strip along the ceiling and baseboard, using a broad knife and very sharp razor knife.*

Step 9. *Use a sponge dipped in lukewarm water to remove excess paste before it dries.*

Hanging the first strip

Whether you have applied paste or are using prepasted paper, the procedure for hanging the first strip is the same. For an illustrated sequence of this step, see the opposite page.

What can go wrong?

If help is needed at this point, it will probably be in one or more of these four areas:

Air bubbles/blistering. Smooth out all air bubbles under each strip as you go. Minor ones will usually disappear when the strip is dry; you can puncture stubborn air bubbles—particularly those under vinyl papers—with a broad knife to release trapped air. Also use the knife to smooth out any paste lumps.

Smooth out lumps with a broad knife.

Misalignment. If a strip of wallpaper is wrinkling or not butting properly with the adjoining strip, chances are the paper is not aligned correctly at the top. Gently pull off the strip and reposition it. Don't try to force it or stretch it into position.

Loose edges. The best way to correct this is to pull the loose edge away from the wall enough to apply a thin coat of paste underneath with a small brush. Press down firmly with a seam roller. Sponge off excess adhesive before it dries.

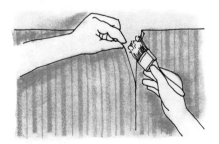

Curling edges. Some paper-backed vinyls have a tendency to curl at the edges. To avoid this, allow paste to soak into the wall covering for a few minutes before hanging. Loosely rolling a pasted and booked strip and placing it in a garbage can liner that you twist closed is a good way to allow the paper to become limp without allowing the adhesive to dry.

Pattern match the second strip

Now that you've hung the first strip, the work will go much more easily.

Paste your next strip, book it, and trim off selvage, if necessary. Then unfold the strip on the wall in the same way you did the first. Gently butt the second strip against the one you hung previously, aligning the pattern as you move

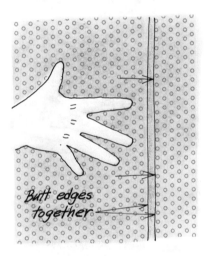

Butt edges together

down the wall. Smooth out the paper with your brush, roll the seam, trim the paper at the ceiling and baseboard, and wipe off excess paste.

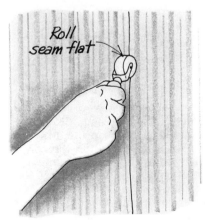

Roll seam flat

With wall coverings that have a texture, it is sometimes advisable to alternate the direction of the successive strips—hang one strip pointing in an upward direction, the next strip pointing downward (in relation to the way the paper comes off the roll). If one side of the paper happens to be shaded a little more heavily than the other, reversing strips will give a better finished appearance.

If you are hanging textured material (burlap, grasscloth, or other woven materials), you may want to reverse each strip for better color distribution—color is often darker at one edge of these strips. But be sure to check the manufacturer's instructions first. If you do reverse strips, butt dark edge to dark, light edge to light.

When you come to a corner

Papering inside or outside corners calls for special techniques. Here is how to handle each situation.

How to paper inside corners

Because few rooms have perfectly straight corners, you will have to do some extra measuring for an exact fit when you come to an inside corner. Start by measuring from the edge of the preceding strip to the corner; do this at three heights.

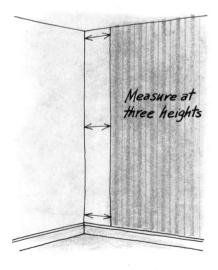

Measure at three heights

Cut a strip that is ½ inch wider than your widest measurement (don't discard the leftover piece of paper; you will use it to paper the adjacent side of the corner). Butt

Making Three Kinds of Seams

Before joining the second strip of wallpaper to the first one, you should know how to make precise seams and how to choose the right seam to suit the circumstance. Following is a discussion of the three main types of seams.

Butt seam. In most situations, the butt seam is the best way to join two strips of wallpaper. It is the least noticeable seam. To make one, tightly butt the edge of the strip you are hanging to the edge of the previously hung strip, being careful not to stretch the paper—*this is important*. Then flatten the seam by rolling it (see page 69).

Lap seam. Commonly used for papering around inside corners (rarely used elsewhere on flat walls),

the lap seam is made by lapping the edge of the strip being hung ½ inch or less over the edge of the previously hung strip.

Double cut seam. Where a wall irregularity will cause the edge of the strip you are hanging to lap over the previously hung strip, make a double cut seam. To do this, complete the hanging of the second strip, disregarding the overlap. Immediately place a straightedge at the center of the overlap and, using a razor blade, cut through both layers of paper. Remove the top cutoff section of the overlap. Then carefully peel back the edge of the top strip of wallpaper until you can remove the bottom cutoff section. Finally, smooth the top strip back down. The seams should butt tightly together.

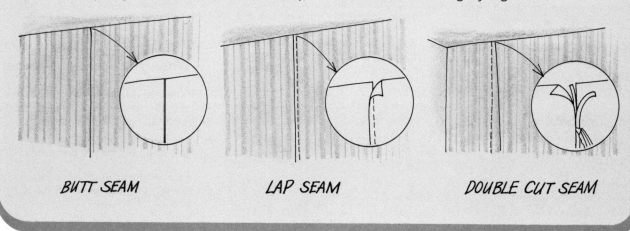

BUTT SEAM   LAP SEAM   DOUBLE CUT SEAM

the strip to the preceding strip, brushing the paper firmly into and around the corner. At the top and bottom corners, cut the overlap so that the paper will lie flat.

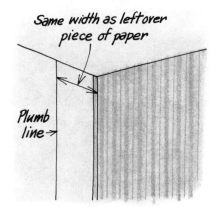

Snip ceiling and baseboard overlap so paper will lie flat

Press paper into corner and around

Inside corner

Then measure the width of the leftover piece of paper. On the

adjacent wall, measure the same distance from the corner and make

Same width as leftover piece of paper

Plumb line

a plumb line (see page 65) at that point. Depending on the direction you are going, position the correct edge of the strip of the plumb line; the other edge will cover the ½-inch overlap. (If your wall covering is vinyl, use a vinyl-to-vinyl adhesive on the ½-inch overlap.)

How to paper outside corners

To paper around an outside corner, butt the last strip against the previous strip, smoothing as much of it as you can around the corner without buckling the paper at the top and bottom corners. Snip the ceiling and baseboard overlap precisely at each corner so that you can smooth the paper into place.

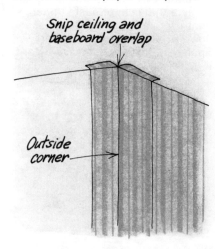

Snip ceiling and baseboard overlap

Outside corner

If you end at an outside corner, cut the strip back ⅛ to ¼ inch. Wall coverings extended to the edge tend to fray or peel, and the ⅛ to ¼-inch reduction will not be conspicuous.

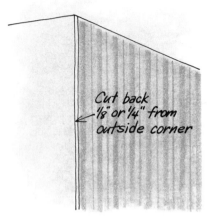

Cut back ⅛" or ¼" from outside corner

Papering around openings and outlets

It is easy to make cutouts for electrical switches and outlets. Make sure the plate is removed first; then paper the wall in the usual way, actually papering over the opening. With a razor blade make an x-shaped cut over the opening; then cut right up to each corner. Finally, trim off excess paper along the edge of the outlet on all sides.

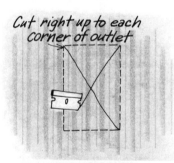

Cut right up to each corner of outlet

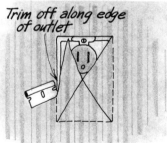

Trim off along edge of outlet

If you are papering around an immovable wall fixture such as a thermostat, smooth the paper as far down toward the fixture as you can allowing the remainder of the paper to drape over the fixture.

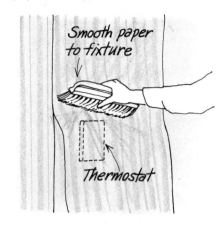

Smooth paper to fixture

Thermostat

Cut a small x in the paper over the center of the fixture. Gradually make the hole bigger by carefully cutting around this x until you can smooth the paper into place; then trim off excess paper.

Trim off excess paper

Razor knife

Papering around immovable objects such as circular light fixture cover plates requires that you cut the paper so that it can be smoothed down (see illustration below). Smooth the paper down toward the fixture, allowing the remainder of the paper to drape over the fixture. Then, from either edge, cut the paper to the center of the cover plate. Then begin to

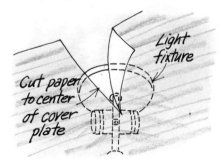

Cut paper to center of cover plate

Light fixture

gradually cut away the paper in a circle, until you can smooth the paper around the plate. Finish

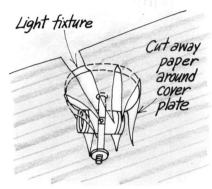

Light fixture

Cut away paper around cover plate

smoothing out the strip, making sure the cut edges are butted tightly together. Trim off the excess paper around the plate.

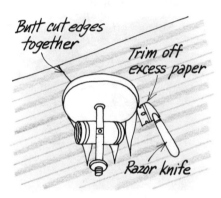

Butt cut edges together

Trim off excess paper

Razor knife

Papering around doors, windows, and fireplaces will not seem as demanding if you think of these larger openings simply as larger electrical outlets. Don't try to custom fit large openings by meticulous measurement and advance cutting—there is an easier way.

Hang the paper just as you normally do but with the following difference: cut away the excess material to within 2 inches of where you will trim; then, using scissors,

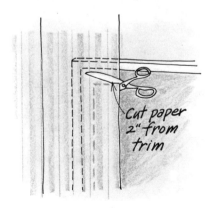

Cut paper 2" from trim

cut a 45° diagonal slit to the corners of the opening. Next, press

Cut diagonal slit to the corner

the wallpaper into place at all edges of the opening with your smoothing brush, pressing out air bubbles. Trim excess material from around the opening's frame, using a broad knife and razor knife. Sponge off excess paste.

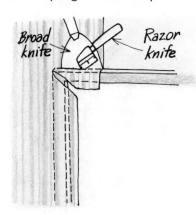

Broad knife

Razor knife

For papering around recessed windows, see illustrations below.

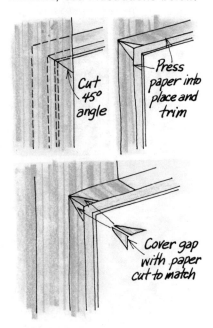

Cut 45° angle

Press paper into place and trim

Cover gap with paper cut to match

How to paper a curved arch

Paper the wall above and around the arch normally, allowing excess paper to hang freely. Cut this away except for 2 inches for wrapping

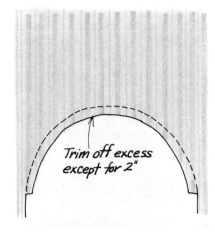

Trim off excess except for 2"

inside the arch. With scissors, make small, wedge-shape cuts along the overlap, cutting as close to the edge of the arch as you can.

Make small wedge-shape cuts along the overlap

Wrap the cut edges of each strip inside the arch (overlapping any pieces) and smooth them into place. Then, for the arch, cut a

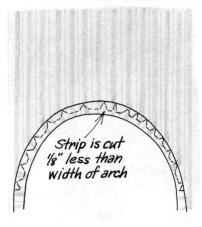

Strip is cut ⅛" less than width of arch

strip that is ⅛ inch less than the width of the arch in order to avoid fraying or peeling.

If your covering is a vinyl, you will need a special vinyl-to-vinyl adhesive where the wall covering overlaps under the arch.

Different wall coverings—different installations

Your procedure in hanging a wall covering will vary, depending on the type of material you've chosen. Following are special guidelines. (Basic directions for hanging all types of coverings begin on page 68.)

Flocked wallpaper

The two important things to remember when hanging this material are to keep all adhesives off the flocked surface and not to crush the flocking.

After you've pasted and booked (see page 67) each strip, allow it to sit long enough to become limp. Then use a soft, natural bristle brush for pressing and smoothing it onto the wall; avoid overbrushing. To lay the nap in the same direction, finish with upward strokes. Never roll the seams.

Lay nap by brushing upward

Though flocks are nearly always washable, you must remove any excess paste gently.

Foil wallpaper

Most manufacturers recommend hanging lining paper before installing foils. Such paper creates a surface that will uniformly absorb excess moisture from the paste.

Some foils must have selvage trimmed before hanging. To do this, place the dry strip, pattern side up, on your worktable. Align a straightedge with the trim marks on one side. Holding the straightedge firmly in place, trim off the selvage with a razor knife, using as few strokes as possible. Turn the paper around and trim the opposite edge.

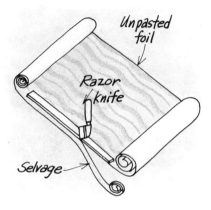

To avoid making scratches, creases, and folds (even slight creases or scratches can greatly impair the appearance of foil) roll up the strip, pattern side in.

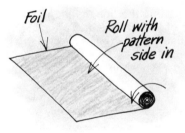

To combat mildew and to provide strong adhesion, use a vinyl adhesive, never a wheat paste. Apply paste to the wall (unless the paper manufacturer specifies differently), being careful to avoid overpasting.

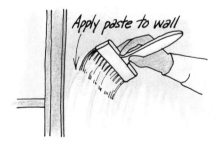

Unroll each strip onto the wall, smoothing it into place vertically (not side to side) to avoid warping and curling at the edges.

Since foil—unlike other coverings—neither contracts nor expands appreciably upon drying, you must eliminate air bubbles immediately. If they can't be smoothed out, puncture them carefully and press them down.

Safety precaution: Foil wall coverings conduct electricity. Avoid touching foil to switches, receptacles, junction boxes, wiring, or any other electrical source.

Vinyl wall coverings

Because they are nonporous, vinyl wall coverings require a special vinyl adhesive. This avoids the mildew problem that can occur with wheat pastes. Vinyl adhesive also helps to keep strips from curling back from the wall along the edges at seams.

Vinyl wallpaper stretches if pulled. If it is stretched while being hung, the wallpaper will shrink as it dries, causing hairline cracks at the seams.

Some people prefer a vinyl squeegee to a smoothing brush for smoothing vinyl wallpaper.

Always quickly remove excess adhesive from the face of this material before it has dried.

Fabric wall coverings

Following are installation tips for fabric wall coverings. (See pages 71 and 72 for directions for working around window and door openings.)

1) Premixed vinyl adhesive is commonly used to install fabrics laminated to paper backing. Trim all selvages before hanging. Then spread paste on the fabric's backing (not on the wall) and hang, butting edges as you do those of wallpaper. To prevent staining, keep adhesive off the surface. If you have to sponge off excess adhesive, avoid soaking—it will curl the fabric.

2) Dry vinyl or premixed wallpaper adhesive is a good choice when you are applying a heavy fabric—for example, upholstery material—without a paper backing. Trim the selvage and spread paste on the wall (not on the fabric). Hang each strip (butting the edges) and roll the seams, being careful not to fray the edges.

3) White glue does an excellent—but permanent—job of holding fabric to walls. For this reason it is normally used for small installations. Always apply this adhesive to the surface, not to the fabric.

4) Stapling is a quick, easy, and economical way to attach fabric to a wall; using a stapling gun simplifies the job.

Seams should be sewn together and staples used at the edges. The staples will be visible unless you cover them with trim or molding.

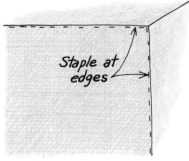

Stapling the fabric to furring strips (see page 24) is necessary when you're mounting fabric on walls that are rough and uneven.

Oriental weaves and natural textures

These nonwashable materials are generally laminated to a paper backing that can be loosened by too much paste. If the wall is first covered with lining paper (see page 57), it will help absorb moisture from the paste.

These materials may be difficult to cut when wet. For the best results, trim them at the ceiling and baseboard with a broad knife and a razor knife.

Align seams by pushing the strips gently with the palms of your hands. Then smooth the material to the wall with a smoothing brush; do not rub the surface with your hands. To avoid crushing the texture, use only light pressure when rolling the seams (see page 69).

Remove excess paste by wiping gently or blotting with a damp sponge.

Hanging borders

Sometimes a decorative border can add the finishing touch to your wallpapering project. Some wall coverings, though, look better without borders, and some homeowners simply do not like borders.

Though borders are normally used at the ceiling line, they can also be used anywhere you want to make a distinct break between materials.

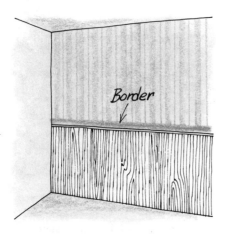

Border

Look at border designs at a wallpaper store and be sure to get the right paste. To border a vinyl wallpaper, use a vinyl-to-vinyl paste.

To paste the border for hanging, cover the entire back with paste and book the strip; do not crease the folds.

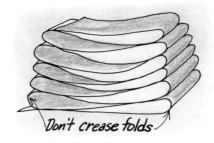

Don't crease folds

To hang the border, begin at the least conspicuous corner. The work will go much faster if you have someone hold the folded

section while you apply the first section. Be sure to remove excess paste.

Protecting and cleaning wallpaper

After expending time and energy in hanging wallpaper, you will understandably want it to last. Protecting and cleaning it will help it do just that.

Protecting the wall covering

Giving nonvinyl wallpaper a protective coating makes it easier to

clean and gives it a longer life. (If you plan to put a protective coating over a porous paper, though, always hang the paper with vinyl paste rather than wheat paste to avoid a potential mildew problem.) Such a coating is especially recommended in heavy-traffic areas—hallways or children's rooms—and around light switches. A protective coating, which changes the wallpaper's color slightly, dries to a clear, washable surface. Don't apply protective covering to newly hung wallpaper until the paste is completely dry (about 1 week).

Ask a wallpaper dealer to suggest the right protective coating to use with your particular type of wallpaper.

Cleaning the wall covering

Most wallpapers come with cleaning instructions; read them carefully. Below are some other helpful hints.

Cleaning with commercial dough. This material is used to remove dirt and grime from both washable and nonwashable wallpapers. Apply cleaning dough to entire walls or rooms, not just on spots or stains.

When using the dough, begin at the top of the surface and work down, using long, light strokes. Avoid streaking by making all strokes in the same direction. As

Make long, light strokes in same direction

Cleaning dough

the cleaning dough becomes soiled, it must be kneaded until clean. After you've finished cleaning, wipe the wallpaper surface with a clean rag to remove excess dough.

Removing stains on washable wallpaper. To remove dirt, grease, and stains before they penetrate the wallpaper, thoroughly wash the soiled area with a mild soap and cold water solution. Rinse with clear, cold water. Wipe dry with a clean, absorbent cloth.

Removing stains on nonwashable wallpaper. When cleaning non-washable wallpaper, be sure to moisten only the soiled area. Using a sponge moistened with a mild soap and cold water solution, carefully blot the soiled area. Then

Moisten only soiled area with sponge

blot the soap solution with a sponge moistened with clear, cold water only. Blot the section dry with a clean, absorbent cloth.

Removing stains with commercial spot removers. You can buy commercial spot removers to eradicate stains from different types of wallpaper. Ask a dealer to recommend the proper spot remover for your type of wallpaper and follow directions carefully.

Recycling Leftover Wallpaper

Before you throw away leftover wallpaper, consider how it can be used imaginatively to create custom touches, give new life to old objects, or coordinate a room's color scheme. Here are a few suggestions you might like to try. Even if none of them is "just right" for you, perhaps they will spark your imagination, leading you to invent some other creative uses.

Enliven commonplace objects. Many things appear revitalized when covered with wallpaper scraps: kitchen canisters, cupboards, wastebaskets, cook books, even the telephone directory. Or use wall-paper as an accent to line bookcases, closet shelves, and drawers.

Decorate unfinished or homemade furniture. Consider buying an inexpensive room-dividing screen

and covering its panels with matching or contrasting pieces of wallpaper. Do you have storage boxes? Wrap them or paint them with a solid color; then apply wallpaper cutouts to the sides and tops. Or change the look of a bland portable wardrobe by applying a strip or two of wallpaper.

Are you handy with tools? If you are, cut out a piece of plywood for a bed headboard, coordinate it with the room's color scheme by covering it with wallpaper scraps, and then hang it on the wall at the head of the bed.

Add an accent to a wall. Use scraps for room borders or to create a supergraphic. Do you want to add a finishing touch to a door, a window, or some object on the wall—such as a bulletin board? Try framing it with narrow strips of wallpaper.

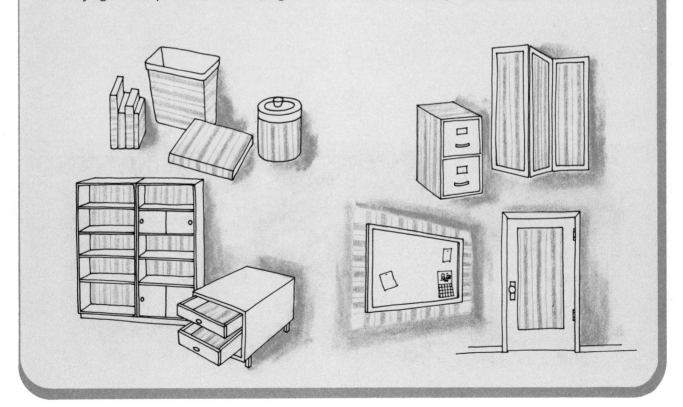

Some Basic Do's and Don'ts

"Dark-colored paint will bring this ceiling down" . . .
"Striped wallpaper hung horizontally will tend to elongate this
room visually" . . . "The warmth of herringbone paneling
will heighten one's awareness of the furnishings."

   Comments like these are typical of professional interior
designers' language and are familiar to the homeowner who
has learned through trial and error what color and material
can do to the appearance of a room. But to help those
who may be a bit less experienced, we have compiled this
illustrated collection of some basic decorating do's and don'ts.

*Three materials fight for viewer's attention; four
subject eye to total confusion—imagine what five would do.*

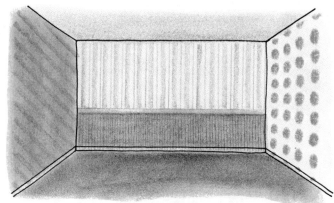

Small pattern shrinks end wall; larger pattern adds to apparent size.

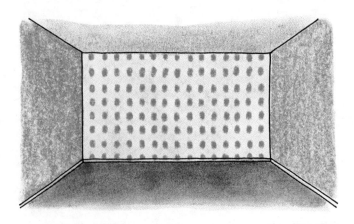
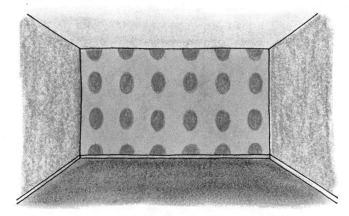

To lower ceiling, use a dark paint; to raise it, go white.

 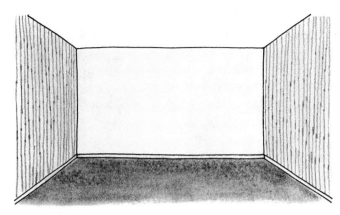

Push side walls out or bring them in with light or dark colors.

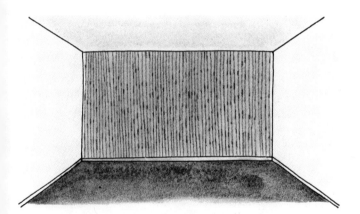 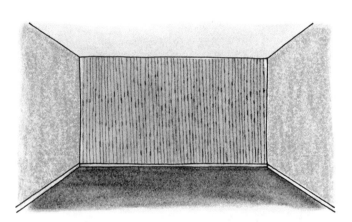

Vertical stripes give height; horizontal ones give length and width.

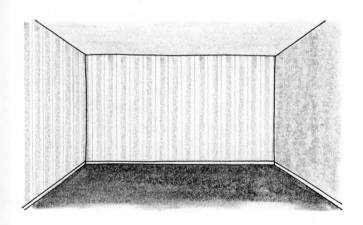 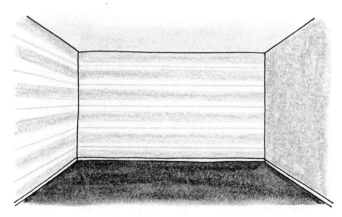

*Unity comes with continuation of wall covering from
one room to another—change may bring jarring note.*

*Which effect is right for your room? Ceiling and wall stripes
running in one direction can seem to make room wider or longer.*

*Camouflage is at work here. Wall paneling added
to door almost makes it disappear.*

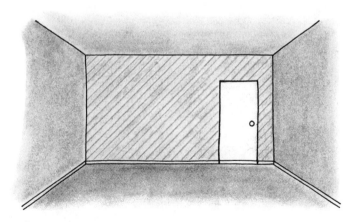

*Matching wallpaper and drapes help to unify room,
set the stage for furniture arrangements.*

 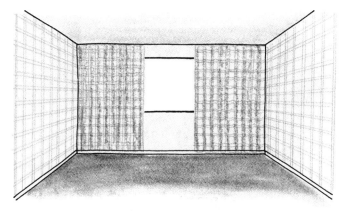

*Mirrors are great deceivers—they can add to the feeling
of spaciousness, even doubling a room's ''size.''*

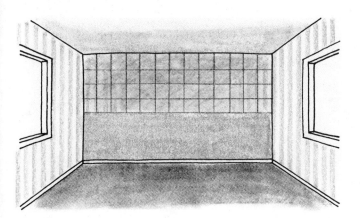 

*Why keep the scene to one wall? Expand the effect
by carrying it on to another wall.*

INDEX

Photographers

Edward Bigelow: 5 (bottom), **Glenn Christiansen:** (top right, bottom). **Richard Fish:** 6 (bottom), 8 (bottom right), 12 (bottom left), 15 (top), 16 (bottom right), back cover (top). **Roger Flanagan:** 11 (bottom left). **D. Gary Henry:** 1. **Ells Marugg:** 7 (top, center), 8 (top left, bottom left), 9 (bottom), 10 (bottom), 11 (center right, bottom right), 18, 19, 20, 34 (top), 38, 39, 54 (top), 56 (top right). **Norman A. Plate:** 9 (top), 12 (top right), 33, 37, 56 (bottom left, bottom right), 57, 58, 59 (top, center left), 60. **Darrow M. Watt:** 2, 3, 4, 5 (top), 6 (top), 7 (bottom), 8 (top right), 10 (top), 11 (top left, top right), 12 (top left, bottom right), 13, 14, 15 (bottom right, bottom left), 16 (top left), 54 (bottom), 59 (bottom). **Peter O. Whiteley:** Back cover bottom.